Exploring the Presence
More Faith Patches

Copies of *Exploring the Presence: More Faith Patches* are available from

Trish McBride, Wellington | trish.mcbride47a@gmail.com

Copyright permissions

Thanks to:

Tui Motu for several articles first published there
Shirley Erena Murray for *God is in the Other Place*

NZ Quilter for the cover photo, and *Spirituality of Quilting*

Mana magazine for *Alcatraz, the Other Story* and *The Story of Matiu/Somes*

Carol P Christ for quotation from *Diving Deep & Surfacing* 3rd ed.

The Tjibaou Cultural Centre for quotations from *Jean-Marie Tjibaou, Cibaou Cibaou,*

Kamo pa Kavaac, Agence de développement de la culture Kanak,
1998, Noumea, New Caledonia

James McNeish for references to *The Man from Nowhere and other prose*

• • •

Editor: Trish Harris

Document Preparation and Proof-reading: Susan Pryor

Design: Stephanie Drew Design, Wellington

• • •

Republished 2024
International print-on-demand paperback edition:
ISBN 9781991027702

Also available:
NZ & USA print-on-demand paperback edition: ISBN 9798878031608

PDF eBook edition: ISBN 9781991027689
ePub / Mobi / Kindle eBook: ISBN 9781991027696

Philip Garside Publishing Ltd
PO Box 17160
Wellington 6147
Aotearoa New Zealand

sales@philipgarsidebooks.com — www.philipgarsidebooks.com

Cover Photo: The quilt is called *Women's Work is Sacred*. 'The doilies talked to me about rose windows, then about mandalas, the sacred circles that symbolise All is One.'
(Photo from *NZ Quilter*)

Exploring the Presence

More Faith Patches

Trish McBride

To my daughters Christine, Kathleen and Gemma
and my grand-daughters Nicki, Caitlin, Sarah, Amy, Madison, Emilie, Abbie, Brooke,
Phoebie, Alexis, Rosalie, Ada and Freda – women of the present and future.
May each of you be true to your own deepest Self. It's worth the journey!

When we lift our pack and go
when we seek another country
moving far from all we know
when we long to journey free

God is in the other place
God is in another's face
in the faith we travel by
God is in the other place

In the hands outstretched to greet,
through the open doors of strangers,
there is love we yet can meet
and believe the Christ is there

Shirley Erena Murray

Contents

Pacific Stories

Thinking it Through

Relationships

And Now…

Foreword

In this, her second book, Trish McBride again encourages readers to ponder the stories of their own journeys by sharing a series of 'patches' or non sequential pieces of writing from her journals, her published and unpublished articles and her poems.

Trish loosely groups these patches under several themes. First of all she describes the Roman Catholicism of her childhood and the struggle of women to be able to use their gifts fully in the institutional church. She then describes events and models of church which she has experienced as more liberating for women.

In the third and fourth sections, Trish celebrates the energy of creativity such as writing, quilting, art and storytelling. This is followed by accounts of a wonderful array of pilgrimages which Trish has undertaken from Crete to along the song-line of the Pitantjatjara people in the heart of Australia. The fifth section includes stories of colonization and injustice and includes cameos of those who have fought for justice.

The next two sections are about one's relationship with God and humanity. They include theological reflections on such important topics as the cross as symbol of substitutionary salvation theology and forgiveness. In the final section Trish shares some thoughts on interspirituality as a dynamic meeting of people seeking to create 'an energy field of compassion to help heal the planet and its people'.

Two qualities in particular shine from the pages of this book. One is Trish's intellectual ability to question and probe theological and societal thinking. The second is her honesty and courage in revealing her own inner thoughts and reflections for all to read. Her intent is clear in her Preface. She wants us to be inspired to ponder our own stories.

In this she has succeeded admirably. These patches contain accounts that resonate with the journey through human pain to transformation. Life presents us with both negative challenges and positive opportunities. In her accounts of her religious upbringing for example, Trish mentions the horror in her child's mind when she thought her fast had been broken before taking communion and conversely the enduring message that God loved her contained in a childhood First Prayer book. Then there is the poignant midlife personal story of death and resurrection contained in the account of her life in myth form. Now in her late 60s, Trish is enjoying the fruits of a journey which not many have the courage to make, that of the deconstruction of death-dealing religious thoughts and the reconstruction of a God image which is personally authentic. She now writes from her heart about 'Life held like thistledown/ On an outstretched palm/Waiting for the breeze'.

May this book inspire many other 'quilts' made of patches of life which have been patterned by events, coloured by reflection and stitched together to form a work of art.

We are God's work of art, created in Christ Jesus to live the good life as from the beginning we were meant to. Ephesians 2:10 (JB)

Anne Hadfield PhD
Member, NZ Association of Christian Spiritual Directors
April 2011

Preface

Many people find the process of leaving the church of their belonging an extraordinarily difficult thing to do. What will I do? Where will I go? Who will be there? It feels like heading out into a lonely desert, beyond the maps and known trails. And yes, it is a huge wrench. And yes, those are valid questions to which the answers cannot possibly be known. But taking one's courage in one's hands and trusting the Spirit to continue to lead and guide is possible. And the desert turns out to be a rich and amazing place, where all sorts of travellers encounter each other. And truly 'God is in the other place'. She is to be recognised wherever there is goodness and love and birthing and growing and compassion for the suffering and dying. She permeates and energises all that is.

These days I use no denominational label. There is a freedom here, and it is the freedom to range far and wide exploring the infinite variety of this Presence, including within church contexts. *Faith Evolving: A Patchwork Journey* (2005) was written to fill a gap in the spirituality literature of Aotearoa New Zealand. It traced the changes in the relationship I had with my God and myself over a thirty year period. It was necessarily about the inner world, and for most of that time I was necessarily mainly confined to home. Since then, life and the world have opened up. In this new collection of reflections, there are themes of women doing spirituality together, pilgrimages, and explorations of the outer world. I was blessed by a two week Goddess Pilgrimage to Crete, a spiritual directors' pilgrim walk up the Whanganui River to Hiruharama, two conferences in San Francisco on the challenge to the churches of feminine imagery for the Holy One, and a sojourn in the Australian outback. Another theme is learning from First Peoples' calls for justice.

My quilt on the cover is called *Women's Work is Sacred*. It was conceived initially to honour the grandmothers who crocheted the doilies, but became a tribute to all women who provide and have provided the basics of home life, and crafted the succeeding generations. And the doilies morphed into mandalas, the ancient symbol that signifies All is One. This book too is a patchwork, largely to honour and document the work of women who live, love and minister in authentic womanly ways. Like a quilt, it is multi-layered. Much lies below the obvious 'top'. The Living Gospel is often like the warm batting of the quilt, not necessarily visible, but hopefully recognised by the substance provided. And as with traditional quilts, some patches are older unused fragments, others are fabric collected more recently. I fell in love with Jesus when I was six, as related in the first two pieces. He is central to the journey still. After several thousand deeply-loved Eucharists in liturgical settings, leaving behind that mode of Presence was a wrench. I have had to learn to recognise my Friend in the breaking of bread with friends as we share a bowl of soup, in feeding the ducks with a grandchild, in the breaking open and sharing of stories. Stories from spiritual direction and counselling, from workshops I've run to facilitate the telling of faith stories, and my own, in this book and *Faith Evolving*. And so I share some more faith patches, more reflections from along the way. Hopefully this book will encourage those who read to ponder the stories of their own journeys!

Trish McBride
2011

Changing Church

Changing Church

A significant theme of the first pieces is prayer and spiritual practice, personal and communal, within a Church that changed so much from the 1940s to the present. Reflecting on 'how did I get to here?' and 'what did I take with me on the journey out of church?' I acknowledge first the influence of women writers on my childhood faith. My relationship with Jesus was formed and nurtured early by them, and has grown through the decades of life. He is here still. He loved and valued the women he associated with in the Gospels. That goes on.

The lengthy years of my charismatic experience were a pivotal influence in my faith journey: responsibility taking, prioritising in life and faith, experiences of beyond-the-normal, all in company with others. Church became a do-it-yourself lifestyle, as it must if there is to be growth. It was communal prayer and practice beyond the Sunday parish doings. And this is where my strong connection with Judaism began, in our recognition that the roots of Christianity go deep into the ancient heritage. Moving past the experience of personal and communal guilt for what Christians have done to Jews, it is a privilege now to be able to share in and appreciate their old and new ways of doing faith and life. Jewish women, too, have been engaged in claiming equality and a voice within their own faith context.

Labyrinths have been an important theme for me. This sacred walk to the centre has been growthful for many in Christians, and others. It speaks of Pilgrimage, and the deep question: 'who am I when I stand alone in my centre, in the Holy Presence that loves and affirms me?' Labyrinths too have been beyond parish, but a more solitary form of spiritual practice. And a recognition that labyrinths are an example of the mandalas, sacred circles, which symbolise the Oneness of All that Is. They 'arrived' as a theme of this book when it was already well underway.

Two Presbyterian churches, a Methodist one, and an inter-denominational chapel have offered hospitality and ministry opportunities. There I've been part of speaking words of life, real words of real life, by women and men who are committed to the equality of all human beings. For this I'm deeply grateful. Within their own institutional frameworks they have claimed the freedom to explore, to be real.

And my family has always been a fundamental thread of life and faith. The nuns who had taught me, kindly, enlivened the images of religious life as I pondered a series of photos before writing the poems. In them I pray as a woman witnessing to other women's spiritual practice. Women have always 'done' spirituality in their own way, though in Christianity they have until recent times been constrained into the patriarchal model in communal worship and organisation.

In the Beginning...

In the beginning were the words...

Friendship with Jesus began with childhood reading. Two women writers started it!

Today by the Church's calendar it is 61 years since I made my First Communion. There are some dim memories of white dress and veil, and of jelly and ice-cream in our classroom later despite post-war rationing. A very clear memory of leaning over the kitchen sink spitting out saliva before mass, as in those days of fasting from midnight I'd been told to swallow nothing before communion. I was a very literal-minded child! Did my mother hide a smile when she asked what I was doing, and reassured me that I was allowed to swallow spit? A clear memory of the joy of receiving Jesus for the first time. Again I believed the words literally. This was Really and Truly Him, and He loved me enough to visit me! It was the first of probably thousands of communions.

A tangible reminder of that day is with me still – a children's prayer book, its still shiny plastic cover featuring Jesus with four children around him. They are under some trees, and the littlest child has picked some daisies for him. I was allowed to choose it from the stall in the back of the church after mass the week before the great event. The pages are all loose now and even the sellotape mendings of my teenage years have given up. The spine cover has gone, the back, once glistening white, is yellow. But the text is still all there, still loved.

The title page reads 'With Jesus. Prayers and Instructions for Youthful Catholics by a Sister Servant of the Immaculate Heart of Mary, in accordance with recent Pontifical decrees'. There is the traditional AMDG – Ad Maiorem Dei Gloriam – to the Greater Glory of God. Those over fifty might remember putting this as a heading in their school exercise books. This unknown Sister, probably born over a hundred years ago, began weaving the web of words that captured me then, and hold me still:

> Dear Little One, Jesus loves you, Oh so much. Won't you love Him in return? Don't you remember how the dear good mothers brought their children for Jesus to bless? That was many many years ago, dear little heart, but that same Jesus from behind the Golden Door of His earthly home longs for your heart today. He longs to take you in His Arms to caress you just as He did those other happy little ones in the days so long ago. Come to Him then, do not keep Him waiting longer. Nestle close to His tender loving Heart.

There are Morning and Night Prayers, and Prayers During the Day, some of them the traditional adult prayers, others in the language of a child. Then the Manner of Serving at Mass, in Latin, with stage directions, right through to the Last Gospel. Next come instructions on the Mass with the text in English. The illustrations have the priest facing the altar, and the chalice veiled to match the liturgical colour of the day. Then prayers for Confession and Communion, followed by the hymns and prayers for Benediction. All that was interesting enough, especially my first introduction to the concept of a foreign language. I loved the sound of the Latin, and later loved studying it at school and beyond.

But then the section that was, and has remained really important for me, a series of what can only be described as scripture reflections, and the laying of the foundations of prayer. Jesus the Beautiful King, The Good Shepherd, Jesus the Divine Guest of Your Heart, and so on through the Gospel stories. Each has an introduction, setting the scene. Then Jesus speaks at length to the child about his experience in that story, about Love, and what He wants her to know from the story.

> Jesus our Hidden God speaks: Again My child, it is Holy Thursday Night. What memories that night awakens in my heart… I was tired, it had been a great day of preaching for me but I was looking forward, dear child, to the evening, for then I knew that I was going to give My Beloved Twelve the greatest Gift that even God could give – Myself.

And:

> Little child do not be deceived by the world and its poor playtoys, nothing is real but God, there is nobody nor anything that can give you happiness. Only here will you find it… You can tell me all your little secrets and I shall tell you mine.

The child responds in a little four-line poem. And so, in the beginning of my conscious faith-life, were words – words that I believed, words that spoke of love and understanding, words that had Jesus wanting my love and attention, wanting me to talk to him, and waiting to respond to me. And that was where my prayer-life began. I have been eternally grateful to that unknown Sister. She lit the fuse of something crucial! Looking back now, it is wonderful that in an age where Catholics 'weren't supposed to read the bible', she was introducing a profound method of prayer which was essentially a form of Lectio Divina. She introduced me to a Jesus who was all Love, with whom dialogue was normal and to be expected. I wish intensely that all children had had this introduction to the Way. The experiences of so many others have often been shockingly different.

The book came with me to many adult retreats, where the words continued to nourish. 'Unless you become a little child…' The Relationship that it began endures, gets ever deeper and richer. I bless the woman who wrote with such insight, such understanding of children's hearts and words, and such confidence in the One who communicates Love.

In the beginning were the words…. And the words were with God, and the words were God.

2010

Stories of Saints

In the beginning there were more words…

And the other woman's writings…

How many readers remember Joan Windham's *Six O'Clock Saints* and its successors, *More Saints for Six O'Clock, Saints who Spoke English, Saints by Request* and several others? They were published from 1934, on through the years of World War II. I read them first in the 1940s, and they still found appreciative readers with my own children in the 1960s and 70s.

She gathered historical research, popular piety, and what is undoubtedly legend into some really fascinating yarns about our older sisters and brothers in faith. From her I learned as a child that saints were real people, as different from each other as chalk and cheese, but sharing a passion to live the way God wanted them to, as friends of Jesus. She locates them firmly in their home times and places, from St Joseph of Arimathea and his trip from Galilee to England, to St Joan in medieval France, to St Rose in 18th century Peru. The story of Rose's canonization seems pertinent to women's ordination:

> The Pope scratched his head and thought. He had never *heard* of such an idea as an American Saint. But all the time the Roses kept on falling and falling; they were getting Quite Deep now, nearly up to his knees! 'I suppose there could be one!' he thought, 'But I don't Hold with it.'

It seems that the author's selection of saints to 'do' for the next book was largely in response to all the children who wrote letters to her asking for their own patron saint to be featured. This was in the days when it was still mandatory to have a name of a canonized saint bestowed before one could be baptized. The mark of the current awful world events is poignantly evident when she comments in a 1945 publication 'every story in this book is written at the request of a child who has written to ask for it during the last five years. I am afraid that it is a bit late for some of them.'

Joan W. has a chatty style, liberally laced with mid-sentence Capital Letters. In one foreword she responds to a critic of this style that the capitals are designed to help the adults who read the stories to their children to emphasise the Very Important words. This habit created a puzzle for me. At six I was reading my own 'chapter' books, and loving these stories. A pervasive theme of all the books is that Jesus's favourite people are the disadvantaged ones. So the Poor and the Raggy duly get their capitals. But for a long time I was baffled by a word I pronounced to myself as '*the l-l-l*'. Even if I didn't understand the word, they were obviously Very Important People! It was some years before I worked out that I was looking at a capital 'I' followed by two 'll's. The Poor, the Raggy, the Ill! That made a lot more sense! So even then she was preaching the Gospel mandate of 'God's preferential option for the poor'. It just wasn't yet called that!

Until I re-read these books recently I had no idea of the influence they had had on my child faith. But now I recognise a profound theology of love, of care for the under-privileged, of friendship with Jesus, of how whatever we do to others we do to him. Simple and timeless principles!

There are also a few bits that jar now, but those were simpler days shadowed by war, armies and the threat of sudden death. In one story she says that Priests have to obey the Pope, Dad has to obey the Priests, Mum has to obey Dad, and Children have to obey Mum. We've thankfully moved somewhat on from there! And martyrdom is so honoured – the Horrible Bits are rather under-emphasised, and it's all Worth It when Jesus and Mary welcome you to Heaven!

The chatting in the author's own voice sites the books firmly in the oral story telling tradition, and they are all the more powerful for that. Each tale begins with the traditional 'Once upon a time…' Her vocabulary is well suited to readers in their early years, with the occasional gift of a more complex word, usually with an explanation: '… everything was in Pandemonium. (Which means that it sounded as if there were Devils all over the place, and perhaps there were.)' Of course! I'd never made that connection before!

And there is a wonderful array of anachronisms to ensure young readers can connect with the picture:

> And he (Gundleus) got all Red and Swashbuckling, and he went home and collected Three Hundred friends and relations, and they all marched back to Gladys's house and Attacked it. Gladys's Rich Pagan Father was taken by surprise, and when Gundleus had got into the house he found Gladys gossiping with her sisters in the Garden. 'Come on, quick!' He said to Gladys, pulling her hand. 'Why?' said Gladys, and she dropped her knitting because she was so Fussed. 'I want to Marry you,' said Gundleus. 'Oh, all right,' said Gladys. And she jumped up on to the horse…

The dialogue is lively, and she includes the Mums and Dads of many of these saints in the stories, saying the sorts of things Mums and Dads still say:

> 'I know Daddy,' said Wilfrid, 'but she won't know that I am going. You'll see. That is,' said Wilfrid in an Asking kind of voice, 'if *you* don't mind?' 'Very well,' said the Noble Lord, 'on your own head be it' (which means if anything happens, don't blame me).

And:

> 'You're too young to go off and be a Hermit.' 'Well, can I practise in the Garden, then?' Collecting these stories and relaying them so effectively to children was a potent ministry, for which I doubt Joan Windham was ever adequately recognized. But I'm sure that others will join me in saying Thank You to her for the Very Important contribution she made to our faith formation, to knowing our tribal stories, to our friendship with Jesus.

In the beginning were the words…. And the words were like seeds, and the seeds grew…

2010

The Charismatic Legacy

The sixteen years
I spent with a
Prayer Group,
later a Covenant
Community, were a
huge influence. I'm
grateful for the good
lessons of those years.

'Come' said the innocent looking notice in the parish bulletin, 'and spend an hour with others in prayer'. That sounded good, and the couple at whose home it was to be were new neighbours, already known through having children at the local Catholic school with ours. So I duly went up the hill to pray. In those days, the mid '70s, 'charismatic' was something of a scary word. There had been pictures of groups of people, Catholics even, praying with raised arms, rapt faces. Quite appallingly exhibitionist, really! And as for the reports of praying in tongues, that was too bizarre for words. Wouldn't be seen dead at anything like that! So I went to pray, and loved the conversational approach to God, the praise, the intercessions, the sharing of needs, the caring. But then the leader started praying in Māori. Then with horror I realised it wasn't Māori at all! Was this the dreaded 'tongues'? No-one else of the eight or so there seemed bothered, and in a while he reverted to praying in English. I was deeply shaken, although it had all been so matter of fact and low key.

Sometimes I went to the weekly prayer group, more often I didn't. After an absence of a few months I turned up one night and discovered it was the first evening of a Life in the Spirit Seminar. That sounded fine – Baptism and Confirmation had endowed me therewith, so building onto that seemed a good idea. Do you want to know God in a new way? Of course! How could I say 'no' to that?

We were coached over the first five weeks of the seminar to pray for 30 minutes a day with assigned verses of Scripture. These were carefully selected, and structured, I realised later, to help us open up to God in a new way. There was talk of 'getting out of the driving seat' of one's life, of accepting Jesus as one's Lord in a much deeper way. On the fifth night the team prayed with laying on of hands for each person individually, and for most this led to a profound experience of God's love and power, and the release of the ability to pray in tongues. Certainly an altered state of consciousness! In the next two weeks we were taught that whatever gifts we received were for the benefit of the community and that we were to go out and use them.

So within six weeks I too was praying in tongues and raising my arms in prayer. And the first time I, with the group, laid hands on someone to pray for healing a charge of power through me to the person we were praying for nearly knocked me off my feet, both physically and intellectually. No-one had ever told me God did stuff like that! God right there, God involved with us in unthinkable ways. It happened many times over the next few years. My palms would get hot, there would be the laying on of hands, normally but not always with a group, and often the person being prayed for would say 'I felt that!' as the charge passed through me to them. Sometimes they would recover from a physical problem, but almost always they would feel better.

Over the next years there were many experiences which were always awesome but became less astounding. And there were the dreams. The first one introduced me to Scripture in a new way. I'd had this funny dream, and woke unable to remember anything of it except the odd sounding reference of Daniel, chapter 2, verse 4. What did that mean? Could it be something in the Bible? Daniel doesn't often figure in the liturgy so I didn't even know there was such a book. I pulled Grandma's old Douay Bible off the shelf, gave it a much-needed dust and looked in the index. And indeed there was Daniel. Found the reference, then sat and laughed – because it was all about this king who'd had a funny dream, then woke but couldn't remember what it was all about…. This was obviously not a coincidence! What was God telling me? That He (because that's how it was then) was willing and able to communicate through the Word? That, too, re-organised both head and faith!

As well as praying, we studied the Documents of Vatican II with considerable excitement: here was the official endorsement of the active role of the laity that we felt led towards. Of the dignity and responsibility of the lay state, in Chapter 4 of Dogmatic Constitution of the Church we read:

> They (the laity) are in their own way made sharers in the priestly, prophetic and kingly functions of Christ. … a strengthened sense of personal responsibility, a renewed enthusiasm, a more ready application of their talents to the projects of their pastors… Through their baptism and confirmation all are commissioned to that apostolate by the Lord Himself.

We studied Scripture, and learned to differentiate between the 'then' stories, the historical contexts, and the 'now' words, the familiar or unfamiliar texts that suddenly lit up with new and personal relevance. We invoked the Holy Spirit, who was referred to in those days as the forgotten Person of the Trinity. And the old Pentecost sequence 'Come, Holy Spirit, fill the hearts of thy faithful and enkindle in them the fire of thy love' transmuted from being poetic metaphor to lived experience. We were reclaiming the experiences of the early Christian communities.

The core of the charismatic experience was of a personal relationship with Jesus. As the sole Catholic in my state secondary school class I had been intrigued by my Methodist and Presbyterian friends using this phrase. Definitely not a concept I'd met at church! When I got to a Catholic college, I asked the RE teacher why we didn't have a similar focus. She laughed and said 'But we have the sacraments!' That didn't sort it for me! But living in the charismatic context gave me this precious gift. It became so normal.

To capture all the learnings and experiences of the sixteen years in prayer group and later Covenant Community isn't possible, but a summary of them could go like this:

> Giving God the prime place in one's life
>
> Discovering that faithfully practised prayer becomes a locus of experiencing God's love
>
> Relating to all three members of the Trinity
>
> Accepting the responsibility to be in ministry imparted by baptism

Loving and responding to the Word of God

Acquiring tools of discernment

Being encouraged to discover one's gifts, so that they could be used for others

Sharing life, faith, material needs and goods with others

Recognising that Church is a do-it-yourself project, not needing a priest to teach, lead or keep us on track, though it was appreciated when one did visit or participate

Being open to sharing faith and worship with people from other Christian denominations

Appreciating the Jewish roots of and influences on the Catholic/Christian Church

Then there were the charismatic masses which joyfully went on for hours. With teachings of depth and substance that lasted for 30 or 40 minutes, a far cry from the average Sunday sermon geared to five-minute attention spans. And singing in tongues – the beautifully soaring and interweaving melodies that transported us to the angelic realms. How could something so exquisite happen without planning or practice? And the Eucharist deeply, deeply appreciated.

With any group life cycle, things gradually develop which don't sit comfortably with all participants. For me the increasing emphasis on male headship in marriages and in the community was a key factor in my eventual withdrawal. Another was seeing a visiting healer at a service in the cathedral 'heal' a friend of crippling arthritis. She walked, and without pain! Alleluia, a miracle! And then there were the exhortations to claim her healing, to hold onto it. But four days later she was in as much pain as ever, with the additional burden of guilt as well, because her faith had obviously 'failed.' It seemed so wrong, and not at all the sort of response I'd expect of Jesus.

I never could assent to being 'slain in the Spirit', the dramatic physical collapse, which people said led to a wonderful experience of peace and love. Nor was I into the prevailing keenness on spiritual warfare – discerning the evil spirits within people and casting them out. It seemed to me even then that it was potentially more useful to own one's own flaws and wounds and attend to them, rather than seeing them as somehow 'not me' and capable of removal by someone else.

So eventually I had to part company with people who had been my family, peer support and social life. This was difficult but necessary. The experiences and learnings from those times have been very formative in my spiritual journey ever since. As I have pondered the hows and whys of those times, Jung throws some light on them for me: that deliberately setting the ego aside gives easier access to the Self and the archetypal regions through which the Divine Presence makes itself felt. That doesn't remove all mystery!

Hundreds if not thousands of New Zealand Catholics and other Christians shared these experiences and culture. Some have continued to be faithful to this particular expression of faith, for example the Christchurch-based Lamb of God Community, of which our prayer group became a branch. Many others found that Catholic parish life did not either feed them or give scope for using their new gifts and learnings in the community, so they left and joined Pentecostal churches. Many moved on to life, faith and ministry elsewhere in or out of the church. And no doubt for many it simply didn't 'take'.

It is only in the looking back that I have realised what a richly formative and fruitful experience my charismatic 'season' was. We were, I suppose, pioneers of sort. Much that was then considered way out is now mainstream. And with the shortage of clergy now acknowledged, initiatives and responsibility-taking by trained committed lay people are obviously very necessary. Was the Holy Spirit running a bit ahead of schedule? If so, I for one am very grateful! Are there more stories out there of this chapter of New Zealand lay church history?

2008

Shabbat Shalom – Building Bridges

A few Wellington Christian spiritual directors were honoured recently by an invitation to a very special birthday party. JoEllen Duckor was turning 50. 'Come', said the invitation, 'to a service at Temple Sinai, followed by lunch and dancing'. I had been to the Temple, the Wellington Liberal Jewish Synagogue before, on open days as I have several friends in that community. So while the building was familiar, being there for a Sabbath service was a new experience.

> I'd been aware of a deep connection to the Jewish faith as the roots of my own since the years in community. We'd been led to explore this heritage with significant energy.

Warmly welcomed, shown to a seat, and given a booklet, we had time to orient ourselves. Rows of chairs, people greeting each other with hugs and 'Shabbat Shalom'– 'Sabbath Peace!' The men wore their head coverings (yarmulkes, or kippot) and prayer shawls (tallit). Some relief that the booklet, and yes, we remembered it started at the 'back' and worked 'forward', had English translations, and in some cases transliterations, as well as the beautiful but baffling Hebrew script. The service had been carefully put together with the birthday celebrations woven in. Perhaps twenty people had roles, ranging from prayers and readings to drawing back the curtain – but that came later. JoEllen herself played a leading part in the service, as she does in the synagogue community, where she is obviously much loved and respected.

During the congregation's time without a resident rabbi, JoEllen has taken on a number of the roles without actually being ordained and formally installed. Two years ago she had a sense of wanting to minister more deeply to the spiritual journeys of the people in her community, but there was no Jewish training covering this ministry. She had heard of the training provided for Christian spiritual directors offered by Spiritual Growth Ministries. This framework has been training spiritual directors in Aotearoa New Zealand trans-denominationally for about 15 years. For a Jew to come into a Christian training programme which makes so many alien assumptions is a mark of true courage on JoEllen's part, and also on the part of those who do the selecting and tutoring of the programme. It has been a wonderful and challenging learning process for all concerned. Last year she addressed the group of Wellington spiritual directors, and they were moved by the depth of her faith journey.

So – back to the Saturday morning celebrations! A first impression was of celebration and cheerfulness in the tunes for the early psalms. Later it was wonderful to see the participation in the service of JoEllen's three teenage children. These New Zealand-born young people read prayers and scriptures in Hebrew, honoured their mother and were honoured in return by the congregation.

We reached the solemn moment where the ark curtain is drawn back, and the scrolls of the Torah are brought out. My overriding impression is of the same reverence that can accompany the opening of the tabernacle in Catholic churches, especially in the old days of Benediction. Both churches and synagogues have curtain and lamp to denote the Divine Presence. The scroll, large, veiled and obviously fairly heavy, was taken in procession around the congregation, and again the familiar reverence of people truly recognising The Presence in the Word, and here they reached out to touch It as It passed. So very like an old procession of the Blessed Sacrament carried in the monstrance. Deeply moving! And particularly when I reflected that this same ceremony has been enacted by Jewish communities worldwide for almost 2000 years.

For the first time JoEllen chanted the reading from the Torah, the familiar story of Abraham being told to leave everything and to 'go to a land which I will show you'. She had a special pointer (yad) to help keep her place, a gift brought for her from Israel. Then she related this to her reflections on her life journey, and her transition from her birthplace in USA to her adopted country Aotearoa New Zealand.

After more prayers, and singing, the service was over. Then came the lunch – and Jewish communities eat with the same dedication as they pray. Tables loaded with wonderful goodies with exotic names, challah, gefilte fish, halva, as well as the familiar, cheese, fruit and cheesecakes. Then the music and dancing – and again the energy and capacity for celebration.

And while the Christians who had been honoured with an invitation were aware of bridges being built by JoEllen's openness and willingness to relate across the ancient barrier, there was another important bridge being built on that same occasion. She had invited the rabbi and members of the Orthodox Jewish congregation a few city blocks away, but without any expectation that they would come. There has been a traditional suspicion between the strands of Judaism, much as there was between the strands of Christianity. But for this woman on this occasion, people stepped across the line, and the Orthodox rabbi made his first visit to the Liberal synagogue to join the later part of the celebration. And so we were all enriched by the invitation!

Happy birthday, JoEllen! Thank you for a special experience of worship and community.

2005

Labyrinth

This walking meditation was another experience of outside-formal-liturgy spirituality, pointing to a newer style of church.

The labyrinth – as I first heard of it – was in Cretan mythology where the savage bull/man Minotaur devoured the yearly tribute of seven youths and seven maidens who were dispatched into its maze of tunnels to meet their doom. This labyrinth was designed for King Minos by the mythical inventor Daedalus (whose son Icarus flew too near the sun and perished) to conceal the monstrous offspring of his wife and a bull sent by Poseidon, god of the sea. Minos' daughter Ariadne fell in love with Theseus, one of the next batch of victims, and gave him a ball of string. By following this he was able to return to safety after first killing the Minotaur. Bull-worship seems to have been a historical fact in Minoan history which throws some light on background to the myth.

After that violent introduction to the word, it was intriguing to hear of a counselling practice called Labyrinth. The explanation was linked to an ancient pattern on the floor of the beautiful 12th century Chartres Cathedral, 70 kilometres outside Paris. A diametrically opposite understanding! Instead of the confused lostness in the maze and the violence and fear at the centre, this labyrinth represented a journey to peace, to an inner stillness at the centre, and what's more, there was no possibility of getting lost, because despite appearances there was actually only one path in and out. The connection with counselling was that while a counsellor may accompany a client on the deep and winding journey, ultimately one stands at the centre alone. And truly God is in that place!

A trip to Chartres was promptly added to my itinerary for the OE. The cathedral truly is exquisite, but at that stage (1996) disappointingly, the labyrinth, tiled and worn by the feet of countless pilgrims, was inaccessible for walking as it was covered with chairs. So I returned home with a leaflet describing how it had traditionally been used as a substitute for a geographical pilgrimage to Jerusalem. I'd only been home three weeks when I met a Mercy sister's beautifully screen-printed pack-away version of a labyrinth at a seminar at the Palmerston North Pastoral Centre.

It was a great privilege to be one of its 'guardians' when it was offered to the women of Wellington at Womanspirit Rising, a festival of women's spirituality, in 1998. Watching women walking the path with reverence to a background of the music of Hildegard of Bingen, the 12th century mystic, gave a sense of time warp. We were in the timeless realm, and the whollyness of the experience gave both walkers and watchers a sense of contact with the Transcendent.

And at Frederic Wallis House, the ecumenical retreat and conference centre in Lower Hutt, a permanent outdoor labyrinth was lovingly crafted and made available to the wider community. It was formed through many hours of voluntary labour and dedicated in 1999. People of all denominations and none came to experience this time honoured walk. Their experiences of it are as varied as the people themselves. And I can attest to the different gift the prayer walk brings each time.

The first time I made the journey to the centre along with a number of others, my main pre-occupation was what would happen when I encountered someone going in the opposite direction. I recognised in very concrete terms that my normal pattern is to move aside, make way for others; and the challenge became to hold my own path at least some of the time. And lo and behold! – some people moved aside for me. The gift was to take that away with me and put it into practice in the daily doings.

Another time as I was leaving the centre to begin the outward journey, I turned to farewell it and found my body swinging from side to side like a compass needle. That was somewhat unnerving, but at another level reassuring that the Ground of our Being does exercise this attraction, almost like a magnetic pole, and we the responsive needle once we free ourselves from the competing currents for a while. We have within us all a need to find and follow this Direction, this Invitation.

And last time I walked the labyrinth, it seemed to be a potent metaphor for the spiritual journey. Within a couple of minutes you are at the rim of the centre – such progress, so quickly! Then the heart can sink as suddenly you find yourself back at the outer perimeter, apparently no nearer to the goal than when you first started. The secret is not to lose hope, but to keep putting one foot in front of the other amidst the turns and twists of life. Then there are the wild swings into new quadrants, or apparent backtracking to the one you started from.

Impossible to see how your present place is located in terms of the overall journey. In and out. Backwards and forwards. Surrender to the rhythm of pacing and turning. Stop a while and enjoy the flowers and trees that surround you, the intricacy of the vibrantly coloured tile fragments marking the path. Don't rush. And if you can't get your bearings, simply entrust yourself to the Way. Acknowledge the dismay at finding yourself diametrically opposite the entrance, yet again on the outer edge. Have you walked, travelled the holy road, for so long now, and in one dimension you are **still** no nearer than when you began! But in another dimension there is the invitation to trust that Jesus, himself the Way, has you safely in care.

And eventually, the relief of arrival at the centre, the sense of 'At last! This is it! I am here!' Stillness, perhaps bringing its gift or clarity or solution to whatever your walk is about. The reluctance to leave, the wish to build a tabernacle, as the apostles wanted to do when they witnessed the Transfiguration – the mountain-top experiences of life – but then the necessity, the requirement to return to the daily and the humdrum and take the treasure of the gift with you to be integrated into what lies ahead.

The longest journey is within. And maybe there will be elements of the old Cretan myth for those who venture to travel inwards. It is not guaranteed to be a journey of all peace and light. There are times when we encounter the demons we have entombed there from our past. And that is when a wise counsellor or spiritual director can be like the ball of string – the reassuring presence which enables and accompanies the way back to the everyday world.

All this from a walk along a patterned path in the ground to a wooden flower in the centre. Many other people have recorded their insights in the book for responses.

In the sunshine and the shadow, twists and turn, sidesteps for others and others sidestepping for you, a temptation to take a short-cut. The colours of earth, sky and waters all blended into one quiet place just to 'be', one with the Creator of all. A sense of being connected in prayer with those who have gone before. We are all on a journey and not everyone is at the same place as me.

The labyrinth has entered the lore of 21st century spirituality in New Zealand as a precious legacy from antiquity and the medieval French church. It has gathered more layers of potential meaning in our complex world as an invitation to the simplicity of a time-honoured pilgrimage of the heart. Come and walk, come and see for yourself!

2000

Postscript

This labyrinth is now in the grounds of Hutt Hospital in Lower Hutt, available for all to walk. It was carefully removed and re-installed there in 2007 when Wallis House was sold. It provides a meditative space for patients and visitors. In 2010 it was the focus for an interfaith occasion, when other faith traditions were invited to come and walk together.

My personal labyrinth connections continued as will be evident later, through two or more thousand years and over several countries. In Crete we danced a labyrinth on an ancient threshing floor. In Cyprus, there is one the same pattern as in Chartres Cathedral in the rich mosaic floor of a 1st century Roman villa near Paphos which I visited after Crete. In the centre are depictions of Ariadne and Theseus and words which relate it to the Minotaur story and Crete. Then there were the San Francisco ones…

Christmas Blessings

Last Advent brought two extraordinary experiences. They couldn't have been more different! One was at St Andrew's Presbyterian Church on the Terrace, Wellington, and the other at the interdenominational Porirua Hospital Chapel. In retrospect they highlighted the paradox of Christmas, one focussing on its complexity, and the other on its simplicity. Both are real!

My quilt and some of my art work featured in the exhibition, and people from my mental health chaplaincy were in the play.

St Francis of Assisi is traditionally credited with setting up the first representation of the story of the manger in his church, to let people see the humanity of the Christmas Event. And in his younger days he was given to dramatic gestures like kissing lepers and taking off his clothes to demonstrate the Gospel and make the watchers think. I surmise then that he would have been delighted with the Christmas installations at St Andrew's on The Terrace.

Judith Dale, a member of GalaXies, and Fionnaigh McKenzie from the staff of St Andrew's envisioned the display, and elicited art works from friends and other artists. A tour round the church revealed treasures that ranged from the traditional to the potentially shocking.

High above the aisle, a life-size figure of a woman fashioned from chicken wire, lay on her side. She had newly given birth, the placenta had not yet been delivered, and the baby hung from a red ribbon. Near the altar was a Christmas tree decorated with AIDS red ribbons, and a black boy doll lay in the manger beside it, to remind us of the children of Sub-Saharan Africa. At the other side was a model of Bethlehem – O little town of Bethlehem, how still we see thee lie – but the town was surrounded by wire and Ken-dolls with guns. There were Three (life-size) Wise Ones near the door – and they were women, who brought their gifts – food in a shopping trolley – to be donated later to the food bank of Downtown Community Ministry. Visitors were invited to add further contributions.

There was a New Zealand summer corner where the towels, togs, flax, pohutukawa were interwoven with traditional Christmas images. The New Zealand theme was carried too by the altar frontal – a painting of a Māori Holy Family.

Behind the altar hung a quilt depicting the four elements Earth, Air, Fire and Water. Of these we are all made and thus connected to the universe, and so was Jesus the baby, the man. Two quotations reminded us of the Christmas invitation to each of us towards inner birth-giving. Meister Eckhart's 'Of what use is Christmas if he be not born in me?' And the Nietzsche words: 'The chaos inside you is needed, in order to give birth to a dancing star'. For so many in the world, there is chaos at Christmas! Entering into it can bring something new to birth!

There was a playtent for children where they could have a hands-on play with a baby doll and some animals, a do-it-yourself crib. And these were only some of the offerings! They were there for the seeing and the pondering from early December, well into January.

From the global and wide-ranging to the simple and the basic: patients, staff and families gathered in the Porirua Hospital Chapel for the annual nativity play. I was there to support a participant, and was startled to be greeted with 'Hi, Trish, can you be the innkeeper?' An unexpected honour! So I was clad in a curtain, and equipped with a lantern, and a copy of the script. I took my seat with the angels and shepherds around the altar. Ian Bayliss, chaplain at Porirua hospital for many years, was the narrator, barefoot, in tee shirt and shorts. It was actually God's version of the story scripted on His behalf by Ian and Kath Maclean, another hospital chaplain. Most of the actors were people with mental illnesses, patients and former patients.

'So', said God, 'when I wanted to send my Son, the priests and important people weren't much use, so I thought I'd ask a woman. Must say Mary was pretty spooked when I asked her, but she said 'yes' anyway. And when I wanted people to tell others about the baby arriving I chose the shepherds. People who thought they were unimportant have been very important to My plan'.

And as I, as innkeeper, prepared for my moment of action, God went on 'Here come Mary and Joseph now. They'd better sort something out fairly soon, because she's having contractions already.' Did my best to make my stable sound appealing, and settled them onto the hay-bales. Joseph, whom I know as a very spiritual person, leaned over the back and produced the Baby which was laid tenderly on Mary's lap. 'Good', said God, 'That was a nice quick labour!' And so we proceeded through the familiar story with the familiar carols interspersed. There were sundry variations and interruptions along the way, but nothing unmanageable. They simply entered the flow of what we were doing together.

When *O Come All Ye Faithful* had been sung, God held the Baby up high, and there was much clapping and cheering, and we sang *Happy Birthday to You*. Then came one of the most moving Christmas moments I have ever had. God passed the Baby to the Angel Gabriel, a woman who has been ill for many years. As she took the Child and cradled Him to her breast, her face became transfigured, radiant, and I could hear the invisible angels singing, as they did on that first occasion. She held Him for a long time… then handed Him on to the older man next to her, another angel, and his face too became alive in a new way. My tears were not the only ones. Christmas had happened before our very eyes! Nothing more was needed.

And the afternoon tea of juice and cake, served as we sat in the chapel became Eucharist. And yet again the anawim, those with nothing, had given the rest of us a great gift in the simplicity of the story and the depths of their response.

To the chaplaincy team and patients at Porirua Hospital, and to St Andrew's on the Terrace, my heartfelt thanks for the gifts of special God-moments for Christmas 2005!

2006

Kiwi Spirituality

For six years a gathering has been held at Ngaio Union Church to celebrate Kiwi Spirituality. This was the initiative of Graham Millar who was minister at NUC for from 2001 to 2006. Four or so times a year, he and a small group of others have prepared an evening of reflection and creativity largely using resources from Aotearoa New Zealand. The purpose is to celebrate and explore aspects of our land, cultures and spirituality. There are opportunities for dialogue, reflection and contemplation, expressions of prayer, music and poetry, dance, and hands-on creativity. Graham Millar says:

> My four years helping form these celebrations was a wonderful way to keep my liturgical interests alive, after the eventual demise of ExAlt – on which more later.

> There have been many celebrations of different aspects of Spirituality in Wellington. Māori, Celtic, Taize, Women's and others. What about the spirituality of our land and its peoples? Is there a distinct Kiwi Spirituality? These are the questions which have driven us to organise these evenings.

The theme for the four occasions in 2008 was a celebration of the Four Elements, God's good gifts of earth, air, fire and water, along with various art mediums. The first occasion had the theme of Promised Land. Earth was the element, and the exploration was of visual art, mostly landscapes. Poems by Joy Cowley, Dennis Glover, J.K. Baxter and Anne Powell were read, and hymns by Shirley Murray, Colin Gibson and Chris Skinner were sung. Those attending enjoyed the art work that was displayed, and making their own mini landscapes with the materials provided around a beautiful construction by Margaret Megwyn. There was time to reflect on our deep connections with this country's landscapes, and to make a personal promise to the land we are privileged to live in.

Other occasions that year featured Fire (Dangerous Friend), Air (Night Music) and Water (Living Flow), and explored Tactile Art, Sound Art, and Movement Art respectively. We played with clay, told fire stories round a 'campfire', sang and danced. True 'liturgy', as this word means 'the work of the people'. All evenings were enriched by powerpoint presentations on the themes presented by parishioner Ian Bolitho. They too are works of art!

In 2009 the theme was Kiwi Holidays/Holy Days, featuring Waitangi Day[1], Anzac Day[2], Queen's Birthday and Labour Day. None of these celebrations was held on the specific days, but were an invitation a few weeks before or afterwards to reflect on the cultural roots and deeper meanings of communal celebrations, and of these days in particular, for our culture and spirituality.

Waitangi and Anzac Day both offered much scope for obviously spiritual reflection. Queen's Birthday was more of a challenge! What came together was a group discussion on the relevance of royalty to Aotearoa, then a consideration of the relevance for us of royal imagery in prayers and liturgy. As an illustration of a trend away from this in Kiwi life and worship, three forms of the Lord's Prayer were used at intervals during the evening. They were the usual modern/ traditional form, Jim Cotter's as in the New Zealand Anglican Prayer Book[3], and Miriam Therese Winter's 'Our Mother, you are within us'[4]… We pointed to the shifts in imagery away from royal power.

We also spent time dedicating 'gold' cardboard medals to unsung heroes in our own lives or communities, and took them away to present to the people. As we heard later, this produced some moving moments. The centrepiece had a birthday cake, tiara and flags – a right royal occasion!

Labour Day was another rich theme. Samuel Parnell's[5] story was told by researcher Elaine Bolitho. Sonia Davies[6] was honoured too, in the singing of Bread and Roses. Rhonda Swenson is part of the planning group for Kiwi Spirituality and lives with a number of disabilities. She spoke movingly about life and work outside the paid work-force, including her experiences of chairing the Disabled Persons Assembly, educating social workers and others about the realities of living with disabilities, and her work as a visual artist. Part of the focus display for this occasion was a quilt called *Women's Work is Sacred* which celebrates the home-based arts of homemaking, childrearing and crafts – the unpaid work of women past and present.

All are welcome to these occasions – there is a welcoming and informal atmosphere, and after an hour or so of reflection there's a cuppa and chat. The present minister of Ngaio Union, Rev Lionel Nunns, says these evenings are an opportunity for a more reflective form of worship that connects us with being New Zealanders. Because the approach and style is distinct from any specific Christian denominational tradition, the invitation to come and be part of *Kiwi Spirituality* goes out to all.[2]

2009

After Christmas

Today, being the feast of the Epiphany, the traditional Twelfth Night, I took down the Christmas tree, the crib and the cards and the other festive 'bits' from doorways and banisters. Four weeks ago a seven-year-old grand-daughter helped me put it all up, and chose where on the tree to put the ornaments and tinsel, and just where Mary and Joseph and the Baby should be in relation to kings and shepherds. Today celebrates the manifestation of the Christ to the Gentiles – that's us! Do we see him?

> All families have their Christmas rituals – here are some of ours. And family is domestic Church.

Taking down the tree decorations was a nostalgic task. The pieces all have a history that is part of the history of our family. There is the startling little green leprechaun, hands clasped round knees, which came with my in-law family from Ireland in 1952. The gold edged mirror with its gold ribbon loop, in which I invite grandchildren to look 'to see Grandma's special treasure'. The little red-beaded Santas made by elder daughter as a teenager. There are three – two are now put aside to give to her children for their tree next year. The red apples and silver ribbon bows are from younger daughter's store, and being housed here while she lives in England. And some recently acquired little silver bells that ring, though not as sweetly as the tiny one from my childhood Christmases. Our family's packing to come to New Zealand as £10 Poms was much more pragmatic – Christmas decorations not included!

Next there's the task of fitting the collection of wooden painted ornaments back into their right holes in the box, like doing a jigsaw. They were probably made in Taiwan. The angel of Joy, the bell of Love, the dove of Peace are gently stacked together. Two black-haired children are tucked in a green bed dreaming Christmas dreams. Then the three little women with vaguely Scandinavian pointed hats, which grand-daughter decided are the Three Wise Women. She has a book in which they visit the Baby, one bringing a loaf of bread, another, a story, and the third a kiss from her own young child. And eventually I take the angel from the top. All so familiar, all with the memories of many years wound around them.

The crib too goes back into its shredded paper packing. Its simplicity suits me well these days: sweetly carved from cream wood, no paint or varnish, relying on profile for effect. Just the basic participants: family, one angel, two shepherds, a sheep each, three kings and ditto camels. The camels have, like Belloc's donkey, 'ears like errant wings', perhaps even kangaroo-like! The only way to keep the family as centre of the scene is to mix up the other participants so kings and shepherds rub shoulders, and the animals too. Power and Poverty sharing space together before Vulnerability.

Before this crib came to me, there was a much more elaborate one, again thanks to mother-in-law. She'd got it in Italy in the 1930s, where the custom was to have the whole village in the nativity scene. When we had the large house and all the children were still at home, it was given pride of place in the lounge, on an extensive table-like bookcase in one corner. The scene was set with a midnight blue taffeta backdrop pinned to the two walls, liberally sprinkled with stick-on silver stars. The angels and the large star hung there too. A hill of books was swathed in green fabric, and a silver-blue river ran across the plain. Then the village began to come to life – there must have been about forty figures, all going about their daily routine. A man fished in the river, a woman sat with her spindle, another carried a basket of bread in one hand and led a child with the other; a water-carrier with a yoke and buckets, women carrying jars or baskets on their heads. And yes, there too, from Christmas Day onwards, was the new little family.

This crib was always set up a couple of weeks before Christmas, with an empty manger – Baby Jesus was hidden 'somewhere safe' by the child whose task it would be to lay him gently in his bed once we'd returned from midnight mass. The kings (all very swarthy), their servants and camels were set up on a distant window sill, and journeyed gradually towards Bethlehem, carefully scheduled to arrive on January 6th. In Irish fashion the crib had then to stay up for another few days so they could 'be there'. From Christmas Day, there would be much moving around of the figures as the news of the Birth spread, and gradually the whole village arrived to honour the Baby. Except perhaps for the supine shepherd who had apparently slept through the angelic summons!

Good memories of all those years, and their domestic-church rituals! Memories from beyond family in my ritual of taking down the Christmas cards from the string they've adorned, marking the notebook that goes back twenty five years , and re-reading the updates of family doings from England, South Africa, USA, Australia and round Aotearoa. It's good to keep connections alive, to have friendships that go back forty and fifty years, to remember those no longer with us! And to value the newer friendships! I was intrigued by a feminist pastor friend's 'Happy Christa-mass', and moved by her card. It shows her own photo of an African mother and child, and was taken following her participation in a US Lutheran-sponsored visit to support the women of Rwanda who are engaged in community reconstruction there after the 1994 genocide.

The evidence of Christmas is now all stowed away for another year in its boxes in the back of the cupboard. Nostalgia prompted by these treasures is wonderful. However for me these days the significance of Christmas is less about acknowledging the Story that happened 'out there', and more about its power to shift our inner worlds. It is wondering what new things the Spirit is conceiving in my life this year. And saying with Meister Eckhart 'Of what use is Christmas, if He be not born in me?' And in this imperfect world, with our imperfect and sometimes painful Christmases, knowing with the atheist Nietzsche that 'the chaos within is needed in order to give birth to a dancing star'. And so we are pregnant, and we struggle, and we give birth to newer stronger selves. Then any engaging we do with the needs of the world will be done more reverently and more authentically in the mind of Christ! Do we see him? In ourselves?

> When the song of the angels is stilled
> And the star in the sky is gone
> When the kings and the shepherds
> Have found their way home
> The work of Christmas is begun.[8]

2007

Untouchable Life

A day, a life
Divided into
Disciplined windows
Through which
Streams prayer
To touch the world outside.
Inside a freedom from
Noise, ambitions
And acquiring things,
A walled garden for the Beloved

Help me take time out
From the scramble
Help me fence off
Spaces in my days
For silence
For going apart
For discovering
Love-maker God
What I mean to you.

These poems were written to accompany a beautiful series of photos of nuns in an enclosed order. A life that, at 18, I nearly chose. But it has been very different.

Suspended in Time

They sit
Absorbing Holy Wisdom
Recognising the old stories
Of God-with-us
Within their own
Those 'then', those 'now'
Those 'still-to-be'
Passing on
The torch of faith
From generation
Unto generation

Sophia, Holy Wisdom
May I believe in
Your desire
To be in relationship
With me
As you were with
Rahab, Ruth, Bathsheba, Mary
And all our foremothers.

A Journey Towards Perfection

Even at play
The concentrated touch
Into the Cross
And Resurrection
Into universality
And the cosmic Christ
Mirroring intent attention
Lavished on the world by
Artist God.

Do I rejoice
That I too am God's
Work of art?
Not inert wood or clay
But vibrant and alive
Co-creating myself
Day by day
Under the delighted eye of the Artist.

Spiritual Crossing

Long years
Of prayer, discipline
Dedication, availability
And resolute faith
Bring practised strength
Deep satisfaction
In a race well run
And an aura of
The presence
Of the World Beyond

God whose name is
I-AM-HERE
Grace me with constancy
And with the eyes
To see you
In the ordinariness
Of day-by-day events.

Waiting for God

It's almost done…
The waiting
The tranquil waiting…
Perfect trust in the Keeper of Promises
Life held like thistledown
On an outstretched palm
Waiting for the breeze…
Becoming as a little child is greatness…
Calm acceptance
Of needs being met
A season for giving
And a season for receiving
A season for doing
And a season for simply being

God of our thresholds,
Show me too how to believe in my worth
The worth of simply being me
Worth that both fulfils and transcends
My seasons of helplessness
Grace me with calm trust in you and others
In all the dyings of my life
Knowing the Resurrection is just ahead

1995

Brains

The Church
Has a male brain
With a dense wall
Between the hemispheres
So connections are not made
And contradictions not seen
The feminine
With right and left
Letting each know
What the other is doing
Has something crucial
To offer

2007

A much later
question: what
IS it that causes
institutional
obtuseness??

Regrowth

Someone deemed the tree dangerous,
Diseased, likely to fall, to harm
They cut it down
But that was not the end
Despite the crumbling rot
The riddling insect holes
It offered hospitality
To fungi, to moss, to lichens
To ferns, to seedlings
As the regeneration cycle moved along
Pine stump now nursery for life
Whose roots will in the end
Reach through to solid earth beneath

And yet miraculously
Between sheltering arms of roots
A healthy seedling springs
The essence comes again
Is church like this?

2007

And from spending time with a tree-stump.

Womenspirit

Womenspirit

I believe future researchers on religious trends in Aotearoa New Zealand and around the globe will recognise the recent shift by women and men towards imaging the Divine as feminine. Documenting the specific and the local is necessary and this section is about telling some of those stories!

A loose committed network of women, most of whom had been, or were still, deeply involved in their churches, did significant work for the women of Wellington from the early 1990s for over fifteen years. I want to honour the work that was done, all on a voluntary basis, as a very real manifestation of ministry and 'Church Evolving'. The aim was to support individual women in valuing their lives, spirituality and journeys, and to encourage the quest for the right to thrive. From this energy came ExAlt, the series of Womenspirit Rising spirituality weekends, and as well, the founding of the Wellington Women's Centre. I discovered ExAlt and became part of these projects when they were already well underway. ExAlt was an 'Experimental Alternative' monthly liturgy held in an Anglican church, formed by and for women, generated by varying combinations of the group. Men were welcomed and valued. It was a lifeline for me over a difficult period. Not surprisingly, there was eventual resistance by the institution.

As we worked together on those projects, the sacred/secular split finally disappeared for me. All is sacred! Soul-mending for ourselves and each other in the practical day-to-day realities is a sacred task, however and wherever it occurs. Sometimes it leads to leaving, as in the story of the inevitable step, my journey out of the Catholic institutional church, written for the liberal magazine *Tui Motu Interislands*. It has been courageous in promoting truth-speaking and challenge – but this story was a step too far to be published there when offered as a response to the question 'Are women in the Catholic Church getting a raw deal?' on the cover of its February 2010 issue.

We need to know our Herstory! Discovering The Grail across the Tasman, and an older woman here who had been part of it was a delight. Back in the 1930s, the movement was initiated by a Belgian Jesuit to acknowledge and utilise the intelligence and gifts of women in ministry in and for the Catholic Church. No longer were they to be simply the holders of teapots at parish functions, the rockers of cradles and the redemptive lovers of flawed men. Then all the way back to Hildegard, healer, prophet, composer, writer and celebrant of the Sacred in and through everything.

The 5th Womenspirit Rising

In 1993, the centenary year of Women's Suffrage, the noted feminist theologian Carter Heyward was due to visit New Zealand. When she was unable to come, a group of women in Wellington decided to hold an event anyway, using the skills and knowledge of local women in the general area of women's spirituality. The first Womenspirit Rising was held at Wellington East Girls' College under the auspices of Wairarapa Community College, which had previously held a successful women's workshop event.

> I was privileged to help organise two of these weekends of spirituality workshops. They were a service to the women of Wellington and beyond.

There were some principles established which have lasted through five Womenspirit Risings, held in 1993, 1995, 1997, 2001 and now 2004. These were that the organisers work on a voluntary basis, the tutors are paid professional rates, costs are kept accessible to all women, and childcare is provided at minimal charge. With this non-profit strategy, funding has to be sourced from community trusts. The Planning Group sets up an organisational framework and calls for tutors on any topics which may, broadly speaking, come under the umbrella of women's spirituality.

This July a very successful workshop weekend was held. It was the culmination of much hard work and many enjoyable meals together for the Planning Group since they first met in January 2003 to assess the energy for doing it all again. The venue as previously (except for 2001) was Wellington East Girls College. There were again over thirty workshops available. There were fun things (barbers shop quartet singing, humour, dancing), health topics (menopause, healthy eating), personal growth (careers, Myers-Briggs Type Indicator) and spiritual topics (an opportunity to discuss spirituality, the pros and cons of forgiveness) and many more.

There were 267 workshop registrations by over 122 women. They paid $10 waged/$5 unwaged for workshops 1.5 hours long and $20/$10 for the 3 hour ones. Childcare cost $1 per hour per child, so the payment of the childcare workers was subsidised by everyone.

Each tutor was allocated a liaison person to be a contact, help set up the room and attend to the necessary paperwork of rolls and evaluation forms. Apart from Planning Group administration purposes, the paperwork was necessary for accountability for funding. We were fortunate to receive a significant grant from Lighting the Fires Project Fund, funding specific to tutor payment from Community Education Centre at Wellington High School, and a grant from CLANZ.[2] These covered the main costs of venue hire, publicity and paying tutors.

So much for the facts! The main rewards of the weekend were in the awesome moments when women found something new within themselves or in their interactions with tutors and other participants; when they spoke of deeply important things for the first time; when they laughed, and when they cried. I call these God-moments!

Three workshops where important things happened for participants were Anna Woods' *Something Spiritual*, Carol Parkinson and Moira McCall-Corlett's *Seasons' Return* and my *Forgiveness: Pros and Cons*.

Anna facilitated an open conversation about spirituality with about sixteen women, some of whom had never before discussed this topic and its important role in their lives. As we listened respectfully to each other's experiences and views a bond developed which in other circumstances might be called 'church' or even 'group spiritual direction'.

Carol and Moira had prepared a wonderful four segment centrepiece with a rich and varied range of seasonal symbols – including different types of lollies for sustenance! We were introduced to the Māori model of wellbeing: whare tapa wha – the four walls of the house of health are hinengaro (mental/emotional), tinana (physical), wairua (spiritual) and whanau (family/social). Then we were encouraged to identify which seasons were evident in these different aspects of our lives, and at the end to take away from the centre things that had appealed to us. My 'winter' daffodil bulb is almost ready to flower!

In the forgiveness workshop we looked at: cultural and religious pressures to forgive on people who have been harmed; the need for justice/accountability; the range of outcomes forgiveness might entail (from full restoration of relationship to simply a deep acceptance of the reality of what has happened); the circumstances where forgiveness is not appropriate (domestic violence, addictions, etc); the conditions for full forgiveness (being sorry, saying sorry, repairing the harm, committing not to repeat the behaviours); and the usefulness of this concept when choosing to forgive oneself.

The Planning Groups over the last decade have largely consisted of women whose feminism has led them out of churches where they had been significantly involved. They have used their energy to empower other women, and raise awareness in the general community of social justice and spirituality issues. This group was also pivotal in the foundation of the Wellington Women's Centre in 1994.

A special tribute needs to be paid to Anne Wells, a tireless worker both for Womenspirit Rising and Network Waitangi – she has been a key person in all five Womenspirit Risings. And to Pam Fuller and Pat Booth who have each been involved in four of the events.

With several members of the current Planning Group indicating they won't be available for another event, there is a need for other women to come forward if there is to be a sixth Womenspirit Rising in another two or three year's time. A letter to this effect will be sent shortly to all participants. Key qualities required: commitment to the spirituality and well-being of women, respect for difference, ability to commit time and energy over a significant period, belief in a collective way of organising and decision making, a range of shared skills including eye for detail, computer skills and financial competence.

Comments from participants:
'A useful, stimulating, supportive weekend'

'Took home much wisdom that I can share with others'

'Congratulations to all of you for providing Wellington women with such a quality and enjoyable weekend of workshops'

'Wonderful women organisers, well done! Life-changing experience!'

2004

ExAlt Reflection

We are picking up again the theme of journeying that was introduced last month. It happened like this: at the pot luck meal we were telling tales about our holiday travels. Pam and I both had stories of our times on Milford Track, and suddenly someone scented a theme for a service. As we reflected on the stories, their inner and outer meanings, and our inner and outer landscapes, we got into deep theological waters and began asking big questions like 'Is God trustworthy?' And if so, 'How trustworthy?' 'Where do we find our security?' We want to give you the opportunity tonight for both wonder at the natural world, and for wondering where our security is based, and who or what God is for us.

My first joyful experiences of liturgy planned by women for women, using women's words were at ExAlt. We took turns in groups of two or three to form our monthly ExAlt celebrations. One of my offerings.

I want to take you to the last stage of the Milford Track, an 18k stint of fairly level walking that had to be completed by 2pm to meet the boat. Torrential rain the entire time – sheeting down. And thunder and lightening. Once you're soaked there is no further problem, but keeping moving is important so you don't get cold. I was doing it with seven friends, but I was slower than the five fast ones, and faster than the other couple. So I ended up walking on my own, feeling really safe because if I got into any difficulty I knew I could wait for the last couple and together we'd manage. It was a real security blanket!

While the track itself was no real problem, the water that poured and roared all around me did pose any number of challenges. Fording lots of streams and cascades, walking up and down mini-waterfalls, wading through little lakes, squelching through bogs, negotiating wet rocks. I was ultra-careful, which made for slow going, but it worked. As I neared the end of the track I was feeling quite relieved and pleased with myself, and wondered how far ahead of the others I was, when suddenly the pair appeared ahead, walking towards me! 'But…! How did you do that?!?' We figured eventually that they'd passed me when I was in a loo about half way along. So for something like four hours I'd been finding my security in an illusion: that they were behind me and could help me out if it became necessary. The real security, the real basis of my safety had been in my own resources and carefulness.

This story started me reflecting on God as Security. I spent many years in a charismatic culture that taught a God who promises care and safety to 'His' own faithful people, God the Rock, the Shelter, the Fortress, the Guardian, the Deliverer. There's the Isaiah reading about going through floods and not getting drowned. Lots of promises!

Some damaging stuff happened to me back then, and I wondered as people have wondered for millennia 'Where was God when I needed Him, when I was relying on Him?' I wrote a tirade of anguish that started 'God, I've got a bone to pick with you…' and went on 'How come, when I put myself in your hands I ended up in his?' I've persisted with the God-dialogue, the God-relationship, but my God image has had to change radically. Was my previous sense of safety, of being under the protection of an Almighty Being an illusion? Had I been trusting an illusory kind of God? So who or what does the real God want to be for me, for us? It took a while before I encountered a God who understands what it is like to be a woman, a God who suffers and celebrates with us.

A researcher once asked me 'How do you know there is a God?' I had to think about that – but what came was that I have experienced the Divine out there, as in the majesty of the mountains I walked between and over in January, the transcendent; I have experienced the Divine within myself in healing, growth, laughter and creativity, the immanent; I have experienced the Divine where there is love, honesty and respect, in relationships. Three ways, which suddenly sounded a lot like the themes of the traditional Trinity.

When our old secure images crumble it can be a fearsome time. Renegotiating a God who makes sense to us can be a lonesome journey. But basing our security on an illusion can be dangerous. Where do we truly find it? Who is the 'real' God? What new words make sense to us when our previous understanding has collapsed like a house of cards? Can we wait patiently for something new to evolve? And discover that we can access the power we need within ourselves?

2000

ExAlt Investigated [10]

It was about 1995 when I first attended an ExAlt service, but I know that since I became a regular attender and began participating in the preparation of the liturgies it became a very important part of my life. Its name came from 'Experimental Alternative Liturgies'. A group of women shaped and participated in monthly liturgies which dealt with the real stuff of their lives: what nourishes, the depths of birthings and dyings, connection with and care for the planet, and our wrestlings with theology, where that is defined as faith seeking understanding. It has been good to work/pray/play with other women who by and large have no longer been able to sustain with integrity attendance at the standard Sunday services of mainstream churches, but for whom a continuing spiritual journey and its expression with others is important. Some have moved further than others from the Christian roots, and that is just fine. We have been able to sustain loving respect for our differences.

We had been based for some years in an Anglican parish, but we were 'investigated' and moved on.

Without knowing a great deal of the parish doings I was grateful to St Peter's for their hospitality. My only awareness of the parish as such was in the person of the minister who sat somewhat sombrely through a number of our services. I had chosen to think that it was because he was thinking seriously about what we were saying and doing, but there was an unmistakable whiff of disapproval. To be at the two meetings requested by the parish hierarchy with Pat, Judith and Marilyn was a good experience of ExAlt solidarity and of respectful process in the way we prepared and debriefed. Before I go on to my perspective of events, I want to honour them for what they contributed. I particularly feel for all those ExAlt people whose parish St Peter's had been for a long time. They feel the exiling at a different level.

I chose to go to the first meeting with the vicar and the two wardens because the August service which had been named as something they wanted to discuss was held on my initiative and with quite a lot of my input. It related primarily to honouring women who have spoken out about sexual abuse by professionals including clergy. I was somewhat shocked at the meeting to hear the vicar speak of the 'hostility to the church' and 'unresolvedness' as his perception of what we'd done that service. My response was that what he was hearing was pain not hostility, and participating in the ritual **was** very resolving and healing for a number of women. If he chose not to participate at that level then, yes, he could well have been left with unresolved feelings.

At that meeting also we were questioned about whether we called ourselves 'a Christian group' and whether we corporately 'believed in the God of the Christian Bible'. The four of us made it clear that there is no group answer to those questions, that each person's belief is their own. There are only individual answers. I had a real sense of there being something wrong with the questions – a bit like 'Have you stopped beating your wife?' A 'yes' or a 'no' is equally inappropriate. It felt like the nearest thing to the Inquisition I have experienced. A lot depended on what we responded! Doubts were expressed by one of the wardens about whether we were 'of God', – a surprisingly fundamentalist phrase for an Anglican context, with its implication that if you aren't 'of God' you have another more sinister power source. She also commented that our use of water on various occasions suggested that we were engaging in wiccan rituals! What about…Baptism? Foot-washing?

It felt good to be able to refer them to their own Book: the wise rabbi Gamaliel in Acts 5, 38-39 suggested with reference to the maligned sect of Christians that wait-and-see could be a good strategy: if they were 'not of God' they would not last, and if they were, then suppressing them would be a futile exercise in taking up arms against the Almighty. This argument appears not to have made any impression on the St Peter's board of enquiry!

Some of us told our own stories of harm by the institutional churches, the why of our being able to participate safely in ExAlt but not in the standard Sunday liturgies. I told them of an image I'd recently seen: a group of Christians gathered prayerfully around a tidy domesticated crucifix, and a perimeter fence of barbed wire where I and others struggled and bled unsure whether we would end up in or out of the church. In their looking inwards they were oblivious – either blindly or wilfully – to the crucifixions being inflicted by the churches. All this too seemed to meet with incomprehension. And after

I'd expressed my gratitude for the hospitality ministry that I'd understood St Peter's to be extending and told how healing it was for me and others to be able to speak our truth in a church building, the issue was clarified to 'Do you consider yourselves a parish group?' They have apparently been regarding us in that light, hence their need to assess our orthodoxy, take responsibility for us and exert control.

We were summoned to a second meeting, this time with the full vestry. It was as though the first had not happened: the same questions were asked, we gave the same answers. When we pushed for justification for their need for our orthodoxy we were told it was because of copyright, and that they would have to foot the legal bill if we were sued! Given that Pat was scrupulously honest in getting permission for our use of songs etc, this seemed both farcical and simplistic. A new question was 'How do you relate to the vicar as your leader and theologian?' Again the sense of 'wrong' questions. My answer, and I think for once the group's was 'We don't'. Other than his silent presence and occasional brief greeting, I'd not observed any efforts by him to either relate or be related to. I'd had this hope that after the Susanna service he might have come and asked some questions about what had given rise to it. But no.

I offered them questions of my own: 'What would Jesus do in your shoes? Was he more concerned with examining the orthodoxy of the marginal people with whom he chose to dine, or with sharing companionship and healing their pain?'

When the expulsion letter did arrive, as we guessed it would, I was surprised at the extent of my pain and sense of rejection: once again the institution that claims to work in the name of Jesus of Nazareth had not followed his example. And so we shook the dust off our feet. Crossways, the Presbyterian community house has given us a warm welcome until we explore our future in more depth in the New Year. It seemed right as we gathered there for the first time in December to note the Advent parallels: our journey too was unchosen, and strangely we had found 'journeying' as the overall theme our services for the year 2000. But we, unlike Mary, had found a shelter and welcome in our time of need. We have come to Crossways as to a birthing room, a perhaps temporary shelter. In the pain is the expectation and the knowing that something divine will emerge from the struggle. And we prayed during our first time there:

> God our midwife, contain in your hands the breaking of waters, the blood
> and din of our birth; then through our tears and joy, deliverer, your wrinkled
> infant community may be born.[11]

2001

Spirituality at Women's Convention

The call for workshops early this year for the Women's Convention at Queen's Birthday weekend 2005 stirred Sisters Paula Brettkelly (Black Josephites) and Marcellin Wilson (Mercy) to offer 'something spiritual'. They were joined by Patricia Booth (a laywoman interested in alternative expressions of spirituality) who had the same vision. They and a later addition (me) pooled ideas, and developed a theme of Nourishing Te Wairua/Spirit. This was based on Sr Miriam Macgillis's Cosmic Walk[12], adapted (with permission) for the women of Aotearoa New Zealand.

The planning team thought this Cosmic Walk would be interesting for women, and would provide a quiet reflective space away from the intensity of listening to the many prominent women speaking about their perspectives on the roles and positions of women. But we were unprepared for the responses from the women who came. There were deep experiences, and tears from many of the participants.

Before all that, there had apparently been some resistance from the organising committee of this secular feminist Women's Convention. Sr Marcellin visited them with the outline of the proposal, and not only did she allay fears of a 'too religious' outreach, but also ensured that a sufficiently large space was allocated.

So in the Green Room of the Wellington Town Hall, we laid out a large koru/spiral with over 60 metres of tie-dyed fabric. The 'station' in the centre marked the beginning of all things 'in the depths of not-yet-time', about 15 billion years ago. Various other moments of cosmic and geological time were recognised. Then the historical record began with the coming of Māori women and men to our shores, and the honouring of a succession of about twenty New Zealand women who have contributed to our national feminine wairua/spirit. These were chosen from a cross-section of cultures and backgrounds, some famous, others not. Each 'station' was marked by a short biography on laminated card, a paua shell and a sprig of rosemary.

The final station at the open end of the koru had, among a heap of pearls, a card headed 'You'. It invited the women to reflect on their own value, gifts and contributions.

The Cosmic Walk was available for the first two days of the Convention as something women could do in their own time. The formal workshop/'conducted tour' of this history of the cosmos took place on the Sunday afternoon. The facilitators invited participants 'to be aware of the mauri/life-force of the feminine in our creation story, the feminine spirit embodied in the women from our past, in you women present today, and in our hopes for the women of tomorrow'. All slowly walked the spiral. A deep meditative silence developed as they rested and reflected.

As they entered the room, each woman had been given a paua shell, a piece of rosemary and a blank piece of paper. Many sprinkled rosemary leaves at the stations as they went, which gave a wonderful scented dimension to the experience. They were then invited to honour and record women who were special to them – these could be set into the koru or put on a special board for responses. In small groups they were invited to reflect on and share something of their own spirituality. This too was moving, as different belief systems were respectfully acknowledged as contributing to this shared time. For some this invitation was an unusual experience and all the more precious.

To conclude, Margaret Megwyn led the group in a dance and chant 'Earth my body, water my blood, air my breath and fire my spirit', which affirmed, embodied and gave voice to women's connection with the earth and with the cosmos.

2005

Leaving my Church

Here is a summary of my own journey 'out'. It was at least as painful as a divorce.

My response to an article in *Tui Motu*, the retiring editor's final courageous call for justice for women in the Catholic Church.

I was for most of my adult life deeply involved in my Catholic parish as a minister of Word and Eucharist, as Catechist for the adult initiation programme and assorted other roles. I gained one of the first Diplomas in Pastoral Ministry from the Catholic Centre in Wellington in 1994, trained as a spiritual director and counsellor, and gained recognition as an Associate in Christian Ministry, an inter-denominational award from the NZ Association of Theological Colleges. All that alongside raising my largeish family mostly as a solo parent. And at that stage I had a couple of great parish priests who took seriously questions I asked, like 'What does God do differently when you bless people and I do the same? When I pray for and anoint someone sick and when you do?'

I spent seven years as a workplace chaplain in an ecumenical context, and worked alongside ordained women from other denominations. There was some jealousy that they had actually been ordained, but also concern for many of them as they struggled in varying degrees with the patriarchal hierarchies to which they had been admitted. During that time I became a funeral celebrant, got involved in the AIDS Foundation, facilitated in-house services for staff to mark restructurings and deaths, and learned from a wide range of people about their struggles with their churches. Each workplace was effectively a mini parish.

Along the way I and other Catholic women got excited about *Made in God's Image: A Project Researching Sexism in the Catholic Church in Aotearoa (New Zealand)*[13] report (1990) by Christine Cheyne, commissioned by the NZ Bishops. A brief flurry of goodwill, but ultimately it was set aside.

In 1994, I participated in research done by Moyra Pearce[14] for a university sociology paper. She interviewed six Catholic women who were in active lay ministry about their preparedness for ordination, should that become available. She concluded:

> Although there is not a lot of optimism that the Church will change overnight, still these women are driven to respond to opportunities to minister in the Church regardless of institutional barriers. With a consciousness of what they are doing, they are creating their own social realities: operating from a different centre, defining counter realities within the Catholic world view.

This paper was entitled *Sub-Ordination, A Study of Catholic Women's Preparedness for Ordination to Priestly Ministry*. One of the other participants later introduced me to the phrase 'circumventing the prohibitions'.

My doubts about remaining within the Catholic fold surfaced in 1994 with Pope John Paul II's conditional apology to women, quoted by Anna Holmes (*Tui Motu* February 10) 'If objective blame especially in particular contexts has belonged to not just a few members of the church, for this I am truly sorry.' I was gobsmacked by the 'If' – how could he be in any doubt? And then there was the total lack of a couple of other traditional Catholic practices: mending damage done and committing to not repeating the behaviour! It was comparable to rehabilitating Galileo and in the next breath banning Anthony de Mello. This was followed by the papal banning of any discussion on the ordination of women. My question became 'What am I condoning by remaining part of this organisation?'

I had worked hard for change, but when the only result of banging one's head on a brick wall is a headache, there comes time to stop. I stopped going to mass when I was going home week after week with a literal headache. The sifting and translating of what I could or couldn't say with integrity was just too exhausting. And I 'handed in my Catholic passport' after some dealings with the hierarchy that I saw as significantly unjust.

In my own ruminations about priesthood, I decided that the Anglican phrase 'the ordination of baptism' would do me! And some excerpts from an article I wrote in 2003:

> When I was pondering the role of the ordained priesthood a long time ago, it occurred to me that Mary, Jesus' mother was the first real priest of the Christian tradition. She received Jesus as a gift from God, made him available to the community of the world, and ultimately on Calvary (as I understood it then) offered him back to his Father. Surely that made her a priest! I then discovered that Mechthild of Magdeburg had had a vision of Mary in priestly vestments back in the 13th century. Women have been thinking about these things for a long time.

Another whose reflections have taken her down this track is Frances Croake Frank:[15]

Did the woman say
When she beheld him for the first time in the dark of a stable,
After the pain and the bleeding and the crying
'This is my body, this is my blood'?
Did the woman say
When she held him for the last time in the dark rain on a hilltop,
After the pain and the bleeding and the dying
'This is my body, this is my blood'?
Well that she said it to him then,
For dry old men,
Brocaded robes belying barrenness
Ordain that she not say it for him now.

• • •

It is a mystery where the men 'in charge' believe their authority 'to allow' or 'not allow' women's ministry came from. The Jesus of the Gospels not only allowed women to minister, he allowed them to minister to him personally. If, as was believed for centuries, sin entered the world through women, and they really are 'temples built over sewers' (Tertullian and others), that could perhaps justify banning them from ordination. Jesus apparently did not share this opinion! And times have moved on. Such condemnations are no longer heard, but the consequent exclusion is ferociously retained!

• • •

Develop your prayer life. Do whatever theological and pastoral care training seems right. Exercise your priesthood as and where your God calls you. It will very likely be outside the institutional church, unless you are very good at keeping rules, and don't mind 'passing it over to Father' at a crucial moment when you have done the spade-work of relationship-building.

• • •

There are many Catholic and formerly Catholic women who would have jumped at priestly ordination if it had been offered them ten years ago. And they were ready, sufficiently theologically and pastorally educated to do so. Most of these, having watched the straws in the wind, and having seen the struggles of ordained women in other denominations, would now say 'No thank you', and continue exercising their priesthood as they understand it wherever their God-journey has taken them.

• • •

I promised myself that I would not again put myself in any situation where a man had authority over me simply on gender grounds. It has been a productive and healthy move. I call myself a hermit now, and minister as and where I feel called, with adequate accountability processes carefully utilised. There was the privilege of being chaplain at Mary Potter Hospice for some months, and I have had my current role as chaplain in a mental health context for over eleven years.

Last year, I worked with an inter-denominational team at Wesley Methodist Church in Wellington on a Retreat in Daily Life. A couple of weeks beforehand I was invited by the minister to preach at the main Sunday service at the beginning of the retreat. After I'd accepted it took me a few days to identify the strange warm feeling. It was, I realised, about being trusted, having gifts, skills and ministry recognised and affirmed, and being a valued part of the team on that occasion. I was even told that if the readings for the day didn't inspire, then please to choose others and the hymns and prayers would be adjusted accordingly. It went well, and the congregation came with their comments and feedback afterwards – a great gift! And a powerfully affirming experience!

The God of my childhood and earlier adult life is differently imaged now, as Source, Energy, Love, Presence, Power. I know She is with me – and my brother Jesus – when I convey something of all this to people and assure them they matter.

2010

The Grail Girls

The Grail – there are so many images from our legends of King Arthur and his knights and their quests, of Joseph of Arimathea and Glastonbury, and in recent days from the novel *The Da Vinci Code*: the Holy Cup of the Last Supper, the container for the redemptive power of Jesus.[16]

> A book about the struggles of educated women to be active Church in Australia between the wars inspired this. Then I discovered a friend's mother was a Grail Girl!

The New Zealand connection is not well known – The Grail is a chapter, not yet ended, in the herstory of Catholic laywomen in this country. It is an exciting story, to be cherished by all those who see the need for change in the Church and work for it.

It was presaged by the arrival in Sydney in 1936 of five young Dutch laywomen, trained in The Grail, an organisation founded by Jesuit Fr Jacques van Ginneken. They came at the invitation of Bishop Dwyer of Wagga Wagga. The Bishop had encountered the movement at the Eucharistic Congress in Dublin in 1932 and had been deeply impressed. Van Ginneken was a visionary who saw a brighter future for women in the Church and a role where they could use their talents to the fullest in the service of the gospel. He told a group of young women in 1932:

> I am convinced that until now Catholic women have been used by the Catholic Church in a totally inadequate manner… Woman's character has been completely misunderstood and the church has been deprived of a valuable instrument for the spreading of the Kingdom.

He had chosen the image of the Grail to represent women's quest against all odds for the Kingdom of God through the development of their own potential and the dedication of their talents to working for the Church. And he made a connection with the medieval times when Europe was kept functioning by the women as most of the men were away at the Crusades.

There was a dramatic response to the organisation in Sydney and later Melbourne in the mid 1930s and early 1940s. Many educated Catholic laywomen were very ready for the concept of shaping their own lives and taking strong roles within the Church and community. The Grail had a political, social and intellectual agenda – far from the traditional tea-making functions of parish women. It was ready to cooperate with, but not be subject to the hierarchy.

The first New Zealand women to receive the training offered went to Sydney in 1937-38, chosen and sponsored by Bishop Brodie of Christchurch. They were Pat Wall (later Matheson) and Marjory Short. They attended The Grail three week long Summer School. It was a turning point in their lives. Pat remembers best the 'affirmation of the female psyche and efforts', the lectures by a variety of experts, and the presence of one of the original English suffragettes, Adela Pankhurst Walsh, one of whose roles it was to judge a speech competition amongst the participants. Pat won this with a speech about Mother Aubert! Political views, let alone action, were not then generally fostered in women by the Church in New Zealand. Amongst other things these courses 'aroused participants to the dynamic possibilities of religious rituals and ceremonies not limited to churches, or limited to the presence of and the definition by clerics' i.e. they were to take ownership of their own spiritual journeys by integrating prayer and daily activities, recognising God in everything. They were also encouraged to do some low-key evangelising – one of Pat's tasks was to take morning tea to some road menders and introduce God into the conversation.

Pat recalls that the committed Ladies of The Grail they had met in Sydney spent six months of each year wearing a uniform and on retreat, and the other six months working on whatever they chose or were asked to do. They worked on university campuses, in hostels and seminaries, amongst others who were prepared 'to live the Gospel in their daily lives'.

Pat and Marjory returned to Christchurch and gathered round them a group of about fifty young women. Then they were ready for service to the New Zealand Church and community. While they were not officially established as a Grail foundation, they were still widely known as the Grail Girls. World War II limited the work that the Australian arm of The Grail could do to develop the organisation this side of the Tasman. Bishop Brodie asked the group to do many specific tasks. They ran a Catholic hospitality centre for soldiers at Burnham Camp during World War II – and yes, some marriages did result!

Bishop Brodie seems to have had a deep concern for the welfare of women – on one occasion he asked a Grail member to discuss the new rhythm method of birth control with women in a country parish to relieve family pressures. He also supported another Grail project: the founding and running of a mid-city Catholic library in the basement of

Hallensteins. This was the initiative of Eileen Webster, a librarian, and was planned as a meeting place and education centre.

There were sports groups, a drama group which dramatised biblical themes for radio, singing and folk dancing groups. Another particular project was support work with the orphans who were being cared for by Nazareth House. Pat recalls that many of the sisters, born to English society class distinctions ('an Upstairs/Downstairs mentality'), assumed their charges would be best served by being trained to go into domestic service.

The Grail Girls challenged this assumption as not appropriate to the more egalitarian NZ society. They coached the orphans in competitive sports and generally encouraged them to develop their full potential. The Grail flourished in Christchurch. The women worked together, and trained others to respect their own gifts, independence and growth, but always maintaining non-confrontational relationships with the hierarchy – another of Fr van Ginneken's essential strategies! A tremendously strong bond was forged amongst the women which has endured through sixty years of faithful work and analysis within the Church. Since the 1980s until very recently up to twenty of the 'remnant' have met occasionally for mass, lunch and community! At an age where most have put their feet up and handed over to a younger generation, Pat and others are still working for a just Church and the wellbeing of women within it.

The Grail moulded the faith, lives and work of these young women – it was a major influence on who they have become. Pat paid tribute by name to many of the other women active in this group including subsequent presidents Cushla Cullen, Freda Khouri (Cameron) and Noeline Edwards (Hall). Pat sums up the Grail ethos: 'the least – and the most – any of us could do was develop our gifts and use them in service'. Many of the New Zealand Grail Girls have now gone to their reward. The group was formally disestablished in the mid 1940s – the war had prevented the presence here of any professed Grail Ladies. Nevertheless, the herstory of The Grail is one to be cherished by New Zealand women who are today engaged in similar struggles to establish a place for women in the Catholic Church which is defined by Gospel values of respect and inclusion. This story must be honoured and remembered!

Pat's Matheson's journey through the 68 years of service to the Church since her Grail experience has included involvement in Justice, Peace and Development and education work, and she is currently, at 94[17], a long-time member of Catholic Women Knowing Our Place. She says that this is where 'women are to be found who believe that membership of the Church requires more than lip-service', and values being with others 'who share in the ongoing struggle for women to be allowed to take their rightful place at all levels in the Church.'

Postscript: The Grail still has a presence in Australia and a score of other countries. Its vision is still 'of a world transformed in love and justice through women's commitment…', and the promotion of a women's spirituality based on personal development and service. A recent newsletter contains articles on initiatives to alert the Australian Government to trafficking in women, Grail-run social services in Uganda, and an interfaith study group. Father van Ginneken's vision is alive and well! Many women have responded to his invitation to serve God and the Church with the fullness of their potential. Has the Church valued this response?

Contact: grailsydney@ozemail.com.au

2005

Visiting Hildegard

An abiding interest in this amazing woman meant a need to visit her, and honour her despite my reluctance to engage with other 'bits' of saints preserved in European churches.

I heard her glorious soaring music on the radio this morning, and it is over nine hundred years since she was born. Hildegard of Bingen (1098-1179) would have been an amazing woman at any stage of history, but that she flourished as Europe was barely out of the Dark Ages is a testimony to the rich monastic culture that then flourished.

A journey across Germany a couple of years ago was steered by a wish to visit Hildegard in her town on the Rhine. Exploration on the net told us that the two best places to find her spiritual legacy now are the Abbey above the town of Rudesheim, and in the parish church at nearby Eibingen. She moved around various sites in the area, as has her foundation in the centuries since. The excellent Youth Hostel at Bad Kreuzenache proved a good base for our explorations.

On the Hildegard day, we drove a few kilometres to Bingen and crossed the Rhine on a car ferry, a delightful interlude. Then up the hill from Rudesheim to the brick Abbey, very visibly perched among the vines on the hillside above. A pathway led up to the entrance, which was covered with a cascade of luscious pink roses. We had arrived! This present complex, we learned, dates to just over a hundred years ago, when a rich prince, himself father of a Benedictine nun, undertook to endow the rebuilding of the abbey on this new site. But it is here that one meets the cheerful spirit of Hildegard still manifest in the smiling and hospitable nuns.

We went first to the church where a wonderful icon of Jesus over the altar welcomes with open arms. Around the walls are paintings of Hildegard's life and scenes from Scripture. Another icon shows Saints Benedict and Hildegard with the family tree/grapevine of the monastic houses founded by Hildegard.

Then there is the inevitable tourist shop – but what treasures! I came away with a CD of her Canticles of Ecstasy, a candle made by the sisters with a Tree of Life design, and a bottle of their very pleasant wine. The sisters seemed surprised to hear she was famous in Aotearoa New Zealand. Maybe they hadn't been around for the 900th birthday celebrations when two Kiwi women Ceridwyn Parr and Danielle Melton performed their moving dramatised version of Hildegard's life. That had been my own introduction to her back in the 1990s.

Hildegard was given by her family to a Benedictine monastery for women and men at a young age (fourteen, according to the biography from her order, as young as eight from other sources). She took vows at 15. This was at Disibodenberg, another town on the Rhine. In 1136 she took over the spiritual leadership of her small community. Her education there had given her a broad knowledge of the bible, theology, philosophy and natural history. Through the monastic life she was also well-grounded in liturgy, the rule of St Benedict and the writings of the Church and Desert Fathers.

Her own description of one of her powerful visions goes like this:

> 'In the year 1141 of the incarnation of Jesus Christ, when I was 42 years and seven months old, a fiery light accompanied by lightning came down from heaven. It flowed through my brain and glowed in my chest. And suddenly the meaning of Scripture was disclosed to me.' And she heard the words 'Write down what you see and hear.'

And a monk depicted her visions pictorially under her direction. From this mystical experience and a number of others flowed her beautiful musical compositions, her three major theological books, her lyrical drama and her prophetic dealings with her order, the church and the world. In 1150 Hildegard and 20 nuns moved to a new abbey at Rupertsberg where she continued to write and compose. She understood God, the world and humankind to be one fabric. The cosmos is God's work of art, and human beings are a microcosm of the whole. Divine Love wills for us both salvation and good health, so one book is about healthy eating and the cure of illnesses. Modern health practitioners have been amazed at the validity of her insights.

She was a committed letter writer – 390 letters are extant, which went to abbots, kings and even Popes, encouraging and, where necessary, pointing them in a better direction! At the age of sixty she went out from her abbey to preach in the market squares and cathedral precincts of at least half a dozen towns. What she had seen and heard in her visions was passed on prophetically to the people.

Some modern commentators wonder whether migraine headaches were responsible for her illnesses and 'bright lights'. Who knows, but the fruits of it all are truly wonderful! Unsuccessful efforts to have her canonized were made in the 13th Century. In 1978 the German Bishops asked for her to be declared a Doctor of the Church. This has not happened either. But her sisters claim both titles for her by vox populi recognition.[18]

More time at the abbey that day would have been wonderful, but we had to keep moving, so it was down to the plain little Eibingen parish church. There was no-one else there. There is a beautiful statue of Hildegarde, pen in hand. Her remains are housed in a gold reliquary on the main altar. It was time to touch it reverently, and be silent before this amazing prophetic woman who had achieved so much for the God she loved.

2008

Stories and Playing

Stories and Playing

There's a whole theology of stories. They are part of our cultural and spiritual DNA. It often takes courage to recognise that we have a personal story, more to begin to tell it to oneself, and more again to claim the entitlement to tell it to anyone else. But then after the story-telling comes the freedom to shape continuations of the story, to change themes, to experiment with new chapters that have been hitherto out of bounds or inaccessible. This section is largely my personal struggle, at times very painful, to learn these things, and I now flourish more or less happily ever after. Many women struggle to discover an entitlement to paying attention to themselves and their own story, but it is essential for healing and growth. Men too! The time comes when we begin to recognise repeating patterns of experiences in our lives. If we're brave enough, and lucky enough to get the right support, these patterns can be explored, challenged and changed. My venture to art school was such a challenge. I'd gone through school and adulthood knowing for sure I could neither paint nor draw, that I simply 'wasn't creative'. Then I began hearing 'anyone can do this'. Sceptical but willing I went to explore the possibility. It was incredibly difficult to move past the fear and negative beliefs. It took blood, sweat and lots of tears. But after that year I can now do things that were impossible before. And from there to the play – enjoyment, pleasure, celebration of colour, form and texture, mostly with fabric at the moment, and its many metaphors. And recognition of Sophia, the Creative Spirit who dances us to new and unplanned places.

It is another layer of awakening to discover that 'my story' is both a unique version of a shared myth, and part of a web of similar stories. That's when the personal may well become political. As thealogian Carol Christ wrote: 'The expression of women's spiritual quest is integrally related to the telling of women's stories. If women's stories are not told, the depths of women's souls will not be known.'[19]

Storytelling and Spirituality

The master storyteller Anthony de Mello once said that the shortest line between Truth and the human heart is a story. And so it is! And the human heart is the home of our spirit, and Jesus called himself 'the Truth'. Whatever feeds our spirit is spiritual, and the work of the Christ in our lives.

We still have in us the DNA of the myriad generations of human beings who learned who they were, what life was about, and the world around them solely through oral story tradition. Eventually came drawing, writing, books, radio, and television. And most recently we have blogs, Facebook etc where anyone can share their stories around the world at the push of a button.

Storytelling is still a fundamental human activity that is taught to us when we are very young, with the time-honoured beginning 'Once upon a time…' It is still the case that just because something didn't actually happen, this doesn't mean it isn't True! We can still access the truths of what it means to be human through stories. They are still a deep way for us to connect with each other in the telling and the hearing.

Counselling and Spiritual Direction are two very sacred contexts for storytelling. People often are unaware that they have a personal story that is both unique, and intimately connected with a myriad of stories of others. Soul-mending and soul-nurturing happen through the medium of stories, as people learn to piece together their experiences to make a more coherent life meaning. The professionals guide the process by focussing on feelings, by asking questions, by offering wider perspectives, until the stories are gently moulded into a new song. Narrative Therapy is a particularly useful counselling technique, which involves creating or recognising alternative stories to the ones that have predominated.

I've come to see the Bible as (amongst other things) a compendium of stories of the people who have experienced and responded to God over the millennia before Jesus and in the first few decades of this era. We find there the template stories of our own lives and know we are part of a living tradition. This perspective opens up new possibilities. And so writing or telling our own God stories is continuing this tradition as well as bearing witness to a precious relationship. It is also a primary tool of evangelism, though in my experience all the more effective for not having changing others as a motive.

Jesus was of course a consummate storyteller – the parables can be read at so many different levels, from the literal, via the metaphorical, to the invitations to what Cynthia Bourgeault[20] calls 'a new operating system' of transformed consciousness. And his story of crucifixion, burial and resurrection is played out repeatedly in each of our lives, until hopefully we come to expect and rely on the resurrection times even in the midst of chaos.

I found publishing my own faith story a powerful way to acknowledge God's varied presence, love and leading in my life. And in workshops, I've facilitated others in likewise recording their God-stories, which has been a special privilege. A soul-work book I used some years ago suggested writing the story of one's ordeals and struggles as a myth: 'Once there was a princess/prince who…' with elements of all the traditional stories of trials, losses, interventions and eventual heroic triumph. This was an astonishingly potent exercise!

I cherish some recent story experiences. One was putting two little grand-daughters aged 4 and 7 to bed, and discovering that after prayers, their family tradition is for the children to tell the adult a story each! A delightful reversal that honours their creativity!

Recent re-readings of the little prayer book I've had since I was six, and a series of books about the lives of saints (*Six O'Clock Saints* etc) from the same era have provided a wonderful recognition that these childhood stories laid the foundations of my faith and theology. The prayer book has gospel stories and Jesus talking about them to the child, assuring her of his love and understanding. The saints were all interesting characters who had in common only that they wanted to love and serve God to the fullest. It was made clear that the Poor, Ill and Raggy were God's special friends and serving them was a special privilege, and that this was the same as doing things for Jesus.

Stories are always political. In Suva a couple of years ago I was privileged to meet Sharon Baghwan Rolls, a lawyer, whose life task is the improvement of the lives of Pacifica women. A prime strategy has been taking a suitcase radio to outlying villages to encourage the ordinary women to tell and record their stories. With this comes political awareness and power to challenge the violence that had been accepted as 'normal' and 'culturally acceptable'.

And in the central Australian desert last year, I heard Aboriginal elders tell their traditional stories of the earth and their way of life which was sustainable for maybe 60,000 years. One elder is also an ordained Presbyterian minister, for whom the story of Moses has particular power: a desert leader who led his people out of oppression to freedom. He integrates his traditional and his Christian stories with great comfort. They believe the earth is held in existence by the spiritual attention of the people. This is a message that is so timely!

Story, myth, metaphor and symbol touch us in our spirits, inspire us, connect us. They are the universal hallmarks of belonging to the human family.

2010

And Then Came the Dancing[21]

Write your story as a myth, suggested the work-book. A powerful recognition of having lived an archetypal journey! As do we all.

Chapter 1

Once upon a time a girl child was born who was destined to sing and dance and laugh. But her parents were a very strict king and queen who ruled their castle and their kingdom without letting anyone have opinions other than those that they had themselves. Not that they didn't have some good ones. The king wanted a son to reign over his kingdom after him but he had to make do with the little princess. He and the queen decided that their daughter would grow up knowing that she had to stay on the Straight Road of Perfection. They did not trust her to grow up and make good choices for herself or even, horror of horrors, make mistakes, for no-one had ever told them that mistakes can be wonderfully fruitful places. They wanted her to grow up straight and tall, so they bound splints to her legs and her arms. She did grow straight and tall, but the splints on her legs made walking very difficult, and those on her arms made it impossible for her to feed herself. The king and queen saw to this and gave her all the food they thought she needed for they knew that was what parents had to do. And so that she would not be tempted to leave the Straight Road, they put a pair of blinkers on her head, so that she could see neither to the left, nor to the right. They told her always to watch where she was going. So she kept her eyes on the road ahead. Consequently, she missed the pleasure of many wonderful places and things to do along the way: she could see them when they were in the distance ahead of her, but once they were beside her she could no longer see them – though she could hear the laughter and songs of those who were, she supposed, taking time out from their journeys. This was a big puzzle to her – how could they be doing all those things, when they too were meant to be getting on with travelling the Straight Road. Because all her looking was ahead she learned to see the far-off things very clearly. She could read the signs and the weather with great accuracy. But not only did she have the splints and blinkers to contend with – the final gift of her parents for the journey was to tell her to open her mouth – then they popped in a large cork. It was only removed for her to be fed. Sometimes she could hardly breathe as she struggled bravely on with the splints, the blinkers and the cork firmly in her mouth. If tears rolled down her face as they sometimes did, though she was quite unable to make a sound, her parents quickly removed the cork and popped in some food as they knew for sure that she only cried with hunger. So she travelled on for many years until she reached the edge of her father's kingdom. And if any passers-by noticed life was difficult for her, they did not interfere.

Chapter 2

She married a king from a neighbouring country despite her parents' displeasure. This time she did leave the Straight Road they had marked out for her as she was very tired of suspecting that the other travellers got to choose directions for themselves sometimes. The king seemed kind and promised to remove the splints from her arms. This was a very attractive proposition and she very much wanted to be able to feed the king as she had been fed, and have him feed her. It was not long before she discovered that he too had a cork. But his parents had made him swallow his and it had stuck so firmly in his throat that nothing could get through to touch his heart. This was very sad as the king could neither accept food from her nor swallow for himself. What was worse, as she had not learnt to take out her own cork and feed herself, she was starving because he refused to give her food. In time they had children, and she wanted a different life for them than the one she had had herself. There were no splints or corks for them – she wanted them to grow up as people free to make their own choices about running or walking or dancing, or talking, or singing. It still seemed a good idea to set them off on the Straight Road, and she wanted them to know their own capacity for clear seeing, so for a while they had blinkers. But because their arms were free they were able to remove them for themselves as they got older. She was proud of them all that they began to make good choices for themselves, and travelled good journeys while enjoying life along the way. As time went by the king became more and more angry and cruel, making her carry heavy loads. For a long time she thought she must somehow be to blame for this, but she eventually understood it was not at all her fault. At last the king died, partly from starvation, and partly from a secret poison that he had been having on purpose, thinking it would make his hunger and pain go away. She was pleased that another part of the journey was at last over, and looked forward to a life of freedom. And those who had noticed something amiss had never said a word.

Chapter 3

Still she was starving, barely managing to stay alive, when she met a magician. He was old and seemed very wise. His kindness in taking her loads from her back, and most wonderfully, the cork from her mouth, caused her to fall deeply in love with him. He promised her a banquet with anything at all she wanted to eat. There were all the finest meats and fruits and candies ready for her, beyond any that she could have ever imagined. He fed her, and accepted the food she gave to him and enjoyed it very much. For a little while they were exceedingly happy. Then she began to notice some strange and unwelcome things: she was only ever happy when she was with him and felt she had been bewitched. And he had become very greedy, and wanted more than she could give him. It was as though a great serpent had wound itself tightly around her head and heart so that she could no longer think or care about anyone other than the magician. This was not at all what she wanted. Eventually she realised that the food of the banquet had been poisoned, and she was helpless to escape from the magician's evil enchantment. Still she struggled on with her splinted legs and blinkers and discovered to her horror that one day when she thought the magician was gently stroking her face, he had secretly put the cork back in her mouth. Then because even after using all the tricks he knew the magician was not able to gobble up her body as well as her mind and heart he got tired of her and left her, silenced, helpless, and very sad with the great serpent still tightly coiled around her, pinioning her arms to her sides. And none of the passers-by noticed anything at all was wrong.

Chapter 4

In time when she was nearly dead, the princess summoned her last strength and managed a faint little cry for help. This was the beginning of the learning time, the time of asking for help with becoming free. Someone who was kind but not always very wise, heard the little cry and took out the cork just long enough to be told the story. But the princess was terribly afraid that someone would chase the magician and chop off his head for having done such a terrible thing. Because she still loved him, she hastily put the cork back in her own mouth in case any of the dreadful truth should pour out when she wasn't looking. Over time she soon met other women who were wise as well as kind. They did not rush in to take away everything that kept her bound up and crippled. No, it was better to sit gently beside her until she knew for sure that she could trust them. Then they gave her two gifts: a mirror and a knife called Truth. The mirror they held up so she could see herself, still bound by the serpent, still splinted and blinkered and corked up. She was shocked by what she saw. They waited joyfully as they saw her summoning the will to spit out the cork, then listened as the poison poured out through her mouth thus breaking the evil spell. It burnt her throat but she felt better afterwards. They put the knife called Truth between her teeth and slowly and painfully she began sawing at the serpent which had held her so tightly. Bit by bit it fell away, leaving her freed but very weak. They tenderly massaged her arms until strength returned and she was able to learn to feed herself with the wholesome food they had brought her – though at first she was very afraid to eat in case she was poisoned again. Soon she wanted to look around at the beautiful place she was in with her new friends – no longer did she want to have to focus only on the horizon of the Straight Road, so she raised her arms to her head and found to her astonishment that the blinkers needed very little effort to remove. She gasped with delight at what she could see. And as her eyes adjusted she found she could use her clarity of vision to enjoy what was close to her, and the wonderful wider vista that was now available to her. She couldn't wait then to unbuckle the splints from her legs, and her friends were right beside her to help her up. They supported her as she took her first few wobbly steps of freedom. They laughed as she walked alone then began to join them in the dance. Suddenly a great fountain of joy and laughter and song bubbled up through the same throat that had so recently been burnt by the eruption of the poison. But this fountain was strong and healing and sweet. She threw back her head, her face transformed with exultation, and as the memories of years of pain and struggle slipped from her, she danced into her freedom. There were those who had not wanted to believe there had even been a struggle, let alone that she had nearly died in it, and did not at all want to hear the tales of her journey. And there were those who saw, believed, understood, held the mirror and gave her the knife. These were the ones who joined her rejoicing so these were the ones she loved!

1996

Toucan[22]

Once upon a time, when the world was very young, before the creation of human beings everything was the colour of misty mornings. The plants and animals only knew who was who by their shapes. Then God showed them the place where the colours and brushes were kept, and said 'I need you to make the world even more wonderful'. They were all so excited and got going with their brushes and had a wonderful time learning and experimenting on themselves and each other – deciding what they wanted to look like, and sharing the painting. Every leaf and insect and animal got to choose its own colours and textures and patterns. They worked joyfully for ages and ages and got very good at it. The world was being transformed into something beautiful to behold, as the dots went on the ladybirds, each tendril of each feather was painted to fit the pattern of the ones beside it, and each leaf got its unique shade of green or red or yellow.

I went to art school in 2004. They said 'We can teach anyone.' Here was their big chance! We were invited to introduce ourselves by way of a performance. This story was mine.

But there was one ordinary-sized bird with an extraordinary-sized beak who wasn't allowed help with the painting. She didn't know why – it was just the way it was. All the other animals and birds knew that's the way it was too. Her job was to carry the paint cans for them all in her big strong beak. She could carry two cans at once and was kept very busy getting the orders, bringing full cans, and taking away the empties to be refilled. So that became her name – she was Toucan. The others used to say 'Hey, Toucan, get my paint next, I need more red – or blue – or yellow'. She did a good job of looking after them all and keeping them all supplied. Every now and then someone said 'thank you', so that felt good.

The other birds looked gorgeous with their new colours. But Toucan was still like a misty morning. She got sadder and sadder because she really wanted someone to get paint for her and show her how to do some painting too. But it was getting too late, and nearly everything was done and the others had all got so very good at it after all their practice. And she was always so busy.

But one day she had an idea: if she could manage to carry four cans at once instead of two then they wouldn't miss her for a while, and somewhere in the forest there must still be a little flower or leaf that the others had missed. She would be brave and do it because it really looked such fun. Nobody would notice – she would paint something little before it was too late, put the lids back on the cans and deliver them as usual. So she collected red and blue and yellow and black because she knew that she could then make all the colours she'd need. By now she knew the colours very well from watching everyone else doing their painting.

Then she hunted for a little flower that had been missed. She had to go off the path quite a way to find one, but there it was. She took the lids off the paint and gave them a good stir with her long beak. Then she started painting her flower – but she made a horrible mess. A very horrible mess! She tried and tried to do it carefully but the paint went simply everywhere, all over her chest and back and tail and wings and face as well. At last the flower was done and that felt good. But what would all the others do when they saw her all orange and red and yellow instead of her usual misty morning colour? So she hastily splashed the black all over her body – that would tone it down a bit, and maybe no-one would notice the mess, they were all so busy with their own painting.

But suddenly they were calling for her 'Toucan, Toucan where are you?', and they came looking for her. Feeling terribly ashamed, she tried to hide. But they found her! She said 'I just wanted to paint one little flower, and now look what I've done. It's all such a horrible mess!' She cried and the tears made an even bigger mess.

She shut her eyes tightly and waited to be told off or laughed at – and there was a horrible silence. But then a friendly owl said, 'Toucan, that's not a mess. You look quite beautiful. Those colours suit you so well. Why didn't you come and help us before now? We need someone who knows how to do it like that.' She opened her eyes with their new yellow and red rings round them, and saw that the monkeys and butterflies and donkeys were all smiling at her. They said 'Come and paint, we'll carry the cans. We can take turns fetching them now. You don't have to do it any more. We've just found a whole lot of new flowers to paint. Come and help us!' So astonished but very happy, she did! And life was never the same again!

2004

The Creative Spirit

It began with a disappointment: for a long time I'd wanted to make – carve – a little woman's torso from stone. This had been inspired by a fleeting visit to Bratislava, the capital of the Slovak Republic in 2003. In the foyer of their museum – and that's all there we had time for – was a tall glass pyramid, and at its heart was a small stone torso. The man behind the counter had just enough English to tell us she was 26,000 years old. Not just four, five or ten

This was a potent experience at art school, of being taught and led, and recognising being danced with. Creativity is indeed within everyone!

thousand, but twenty six thousand years old! The imagination boggled, that human beings, that long ago in Eastern Europe, had the reverence for the female form and the skills to produce this simple little goddess figure.

I wanted to make one too, and here was my big chance. I was a beginning artist at art school, with a piece of white Oamaru stone in my hand, and rasp, chisel and other tools all available, garbed in an old shirt and a dust mask. The initial enthusiasm turned to frustration and then to sadness. My hands weren't strong enough to hold the stone effectively against the tools, and the mask made my glasses fog up. I could either breathe or see – but not both at once! The tutor suggested going back to working with clay. I was reluctant to give up, but it seemed an ok idea, though I had no idea what else to make.

It had to be something from back then though, and within my *very* limited skill range – a stone circle suddenly seemed a possibility. Even I could manage a circle of clay stones!

After forming the first couple, I realised which stone circle it was – the one called Long Meg and her Daughters in North Yorkshire, England which I'd visited on the same trip. So a stylised and vaguely feminine Long Meg was smoothed and set outside where the circle would be, then I continued making more stones. Suddenly they began shaping themselves into little women, at first barely emerging from their stones, like little gingerbread people, then becoming more developed until the last five were actually dancing. Their feet stamped, their arms waved, and with the thirteenth, the circle was complete, and Long Meg looking lovingly on from beyond the circumference.

Suddenly the penny dropped: I had just unwittingly achieved with clay what had been impossible for me in the other medium: here were women who had emerged from stones! And it had been through no conscious plan of mine. I was startled into knowing that there was 'something going on' that was not of my own making. And the next jolt of realisation was the parallel to therapy – both my own, and what I offer others: the process of extricating ourselves from constraints, from all that prevents us dancing. This stone circle was developing an eloquent life of its own, and I was simply the observer. Eventually there they were, a complete circle, not artistically sophisticated, but astonishing – and both mine and not mine!

For two weeks they stood drying on their board off-cut on a shelf. 'Did I do that?' I wondered each time I passed them. 'How did I do that?' A mystery! Then finally it was time for them to be fired in the communal kiln. The tutor was pretty sure they'd survive the process. I hoped so. I loved them so much. But when we went a couple of days later, I was heart-broken to find the dancing women in bits – tiny arms and heads and legs and dismembered bodies. Had someone dropped them? Or had they not withstood the fire after all? I'd have despairingly swept the lot into the rubbish bin, but again some guidance from the tutor. 'You know, you could mend these' he said thoughtfully. So we gathered up the baked fragments into a plastic bag, and I took them home, still grieving.

It was a major effort to get out the superglue, and to work out the jigsaw of which bits belonged to whom. The position and shape of the joints did not lend themselves to being propped up to bond, so it was a case of holding two tiny parts together until they had healed. As often, and for as long as it took to restore them to themselves and to the circle. Much hope and patience needed! The glued scars were still visible, one dancer was still minus an arm, but they were back together and celebrating. I was too!

And again they became eloquent – a poem this time:

> Emerging from primal constraints
> Becoming fragile
> Broken by fire or careless knocks
>
> Mended with time, care and holding
> Here are women
> ***Dancing anyway!***

I painted their board green, blue-tacked them to it to give them a bit more stability, typed out their poem and glued it with them. And wondered again at the journey of the process, and the discoveries that had attended their creation! Still it awes me! They dance on. Blessed be the Creative Spirit!

2007

The Spirituality of Quilting[23]

What is it about quilting that grabs us, that does us good? Having pondered this for a few years while I've indulged my own learning and doing, here are some of the answers that I've found.

It is about beauty, complexity, giving gifts of warmth and comfort. It is about artistry and creativity. It is about bringing fragments together to make a coherent whole. It is about patience and going step by step, each one taking as long as it needs. It is about the meditative practice of simple stitching and stitching and stitching. It can be done alone or in company, and great among quilters is the generous sharing of ideas, techniques and bits of fabric.

> If, as a wise man said, 'Spirituality is the loves which give meaning to our lives,' then the women (and the men) who love quilting are engaged in a spiritual practice.

I didn't recognise it as quilting at the time, but my two first quilts back in the 1970s were simply to keep my children warm in bed. My frugal Depression-educated mother showed me how to jigsaw woolly jerseys and cardigans past their use-by date between two old curtains, and sew the sandwich together. I was startled to see a very similar cover hailed in an Australian magazine recently as a treasure, a museum piece. She also showed me how to make bags about 15cm by 20cm from scraps left from making kids' clothes. Into each went a shredded pair of nylons – before pantyhose! They got joined together, and formed an eiderdown of sorts. It was in the days before duvets too! Re-use, recycle was a necessity!

Much, much later I bought a few bits of fabric from the Salvation Army bin, the templates for Storm at Sea, and did my first intentional patchwork, a floor cushion. I still love it, and grandchildren now enjoy lounging on it. Eventually I was able to buy some bits of new fabric, and really get into quilting, recognising that being able to at last afford doing this is a privilege many women don't have. At first I was meticulous, following other people's designs, and being thrilled with the predicted and predictable results.

Later again came the urge to design my own quilts, and the first step for this was a Crazy Quilt course. I loved the opulence, the variety of fabrics, new techniques, the over-the top use of all the little bits and bobs that my magpie self had been saving for years. And its uniqueness! Four panels represent the four elements Earth, Air, Fire and Water, with colours, shapes and textures. A riot of colour and sparkle! And it had a spiritual significance for me. These elements are what we are all made of, and there's a women's chant that goes 'Earth my body, water my blood, air my breath, and fire my spirit'. My quilt expresses all this. It hung for some months behind the altar in a Wellington church.

In 2006 I visited Crete to honour Minoan women from 5000 years ago, our foremothers who were spinners and weavers, and they were in turn descended from the original women who spun and wove maybe 20,000 years ago. We are in a long tradition! And I discovered a deep reverence for the work women have done in developing both useful and decorative fabric arts.

This led to a major quilt project, the designing of which was a significant challenge. To honour our grandmothers who made crochet doilies, I collected a couple of dozen – mostly from friends and op shops. I knew I wanted to display them on plain panels. They started talking to me about rose windows, those glorious art works in medieval cathedrals, so I knew to surround the panels with black to indicate stained glass. And the panel colours had to be vibrant, luminous.

Then they talked about being mandalas as well, the sacred circles that indicate All is One. Most of the doilies are hand made, but a few could have been made on machines by Chinese women in sweatshops. They too are honoured, as are all who raise children and make homes. The quilt is called *Women's Work is Sacred*.

A friend brought her mother's carefully stored treasure trove of doilies, to offer them for another project. They were yellowed white, hand-made in India over fifty years ago. So their makers also became a focus of a project. There is a set of nineteen matching mats, one large, and three different sized sets of six. They soaked to gleaming white, and now feature on a quilted hexagonal wall hanging, much to my friend's delight, a potent connection to her missionary mother and the women of her birthplace. She calls it Indian Cosmic Energy.

So quilting connects and bonds women across time and distance. A present day demonstration of this is the annual gift to the two Wellington Women's Refuges of quilts by a dedicated group from Wellington Quilters' Guild. They have been doing this for about 12 years. Women come to Refuge for safety, comfort and hopefully a new life. They find a new quilt on their bed, and can take these with them when they leave. About a hundred quilts made as gifts of comfort and support were handed over in June.

Women's spirituality is often about connecting, creating, beauty, shaping, nurturing, giving, loving, and trying to make sense of the life we lead. This all goes into our quilting as we simply cut and stitch and give with love!

2010

Pilgrimages near and far

Pilgrimages near and far

The tradition of travelling to sacred places for a spiritual deepening is very ancient. The Greeks and Romans honoured their sacred sites and travelled dedicated journeys to visit them. They were not the first. It is giving significant time to spiritually-aware travel with its pleasures and hardships, usually in the company of others. Travels in recent years have taken me to places sacred to my own tradition, and to those of others. Places where people have lived and died in extraordinary ways, 'thin' places where the Sacred breaks through. People remember and visit to see whether they can experience some of that greater reality for themselves. So I visited holy places in Europe, my birthplace in England, Poland (especially Auschwitz), the Crete of the ancient matrifocal civilisation, and then to San Francisco. Hildegard could well have appeared in this section too. Closer to home were visits to an Aboriginal community in outback Australia, and a three day walk up the Whanganui River with other spiritual directors to our own Jerusalem – Hiruhārama.

The Crete trip was as pivotal in its way as the years of charismatic experience. I was with other women who were also re-working, re-wording and blending their Christian backgrounds with consciousness of the ancient tradition of the Divine Feminine, the Great Mother Goddess. We were at many different points within that matrix. One of the wonderful things about women's spirituality is the acceptance of differences in understanding. It is so respectful! When the duality of 'right' and 'wrong' has been set aside, we can travel together and listen to each other in peace. Because of the importance of that journey I've retained a degree of detail beyond that of other stories. The daily travel with its trivia, challenges and irritations was as important, as sacred as the destinations! The noticing, the awareness – Goddess/God speaks through the mundane as well as the dramatic.

Ultimately, of course, 'the longest journey is within'. I had a sense of that pilgrimage to be undertaken a long time ago. Would I use the same words now? Probably not, but the inner pilgrimage is still as crucially important. If we don't find Her vibrantly active in the depths of our own experience, where else will we find Her?

Pilgrimage

Pilgrims flock to where it all began
To kneel where lifeless corpse
Enbalmed enshrouded briefly lay
And to the marks along the way
But here's the miracle!
Day by day I become

- the manger strawed and poor
  where perfect baby beauty slept

- the Nazareth home rejoicing in growth
  of grace and wisdom in the God-man-child

- the wedding place at Cana whose need was met
  by strength and sparkle of finest wine

- the synagogue wherein the Word
  proclaimed the Word's fulfilment now

- the storm-rocked boat (dare I trust a sleeping Lord?)

- the Martha-Mary home he loved to visit

- the many-splendoured temple, House of awe

- Upper Room where bread became God

- garden where he suffered, bled, obeyed

- courtyard that saw him flayed and mocked and crowned

- Calvary, though in me he lives

- house where doubt was quenched by nail-marks shown
  where rushing winds and fiery tongues proclaimed the
  Spirit's power

- the throne on which the King of glory sits,

Lord of stars and sun and moon.
Within my hollowness is the Living God
Come, let us adore him!

1984

In the days of family raising and very limited resources, lots of people I knew seemed to be heading off on exciting pilgrimages to the Holy Places. I discovered inner journeys.

Sacred Stones

On a three month odyssey around Europe it was unsurprising that themes should develop. One constant that became apparent early was 'stones' – or maybe 'stone'. But then constancy is the nature of stone! This is how human beings have left visible traces of their lives, their technical abilities and their yearning for the sacred for the last five millennia. For at least that long human beings have fashioned the hard bone of the earth into tools, shelter and sacred places. There are the stones made into homes and larger buildings, those carved into astonishing lace cathedrals, stones that mark the graves of ancestors, milestones and mill stones, and stones placed by the long-gone ones for their ritual, scientific and community uses.

> But eventually my turn came to travel. A fascination with the Old Ones just can't be explored in the same way in Aotearoa New Zealand.

Stone circles exercise a magnetic attraction for me, as for many. There are a number in the North of England and the first two I visited were the Swinside Circle in Cumbria, and Long Meg and her Daughters in West Yorkshire. We reached the first after a walk up a farm hillside – 55 stones making a circle 27 metres in diameter. It probably dates from about the time Abraham and Sarah were leaving their security to journey in faith. What were the names of the ancestors who prepared this ground for these stones, then arranged them in the circle? Was it their community centre, their place of worship, their 'church'? It seemed respectful to walk round the outside of the circle in acknowledgement before entering. Then I stood in the centre and was transported back in time to when the old ones danced and sang round their fire here. Of this I am sure, that the women, men and children who came together there were more like us than unlike us.

And a similar experience with Long Meg, near the village of Little Salkeld. 'She' is a huge dressed stone which stands outside the circle of her 59 remaining 'daughters'. To trace with a finger the spiral carvings on Meg is to literally be in touch with one who executed the pattern. What might it have meant? It's likely that some of my blood ancestors were participants in the life of this place. I hope they were well clad in layers of skins to protect them against the biting cold!

Later I visited Avebury, near Stonehenge, a site where there are the remains of an astonishingly complex ordering of stones – interweaving circles, avenues, a long barrow (burial site), and Silbury Hill, the largest man-made sacred mountain in Europe. The geometry of the site, which covers over 11 hectares, has been the subject of speculations which connect it to the pyramids of Egypt. It dates from about 2600 BC.

Half way from there to here time-wise is Hadrian's Wall, built in 121-122 AD across the north of England as a frontier of the Roman Empire to keep out Scottish invaders. Again I felt for the builders with the climate as I experienced it: Roman soldiers from various parts of the Empire, who shaped each block of stone for the outside layer of masonry, then filled it with its rougher core. Nothing obviously sacred here, but when we headed down the hill to see the 12th century Lanercost church and priory we were confronted by some 900 year old recycling. As Hadrian's Wall gradually collapsed and as building techniques developed, the locals of 1166 did the obvious thing, and brought the worked stone blocks down to build their church and priory. Some of the stones in the 'new' buildings still bear the inscriptions carved by the Roman wall builders who had shaped them.

This recycling of Roman materials was also evident at Canterbury where Roman bricks had been used to build the priory of St Augustine's Abbey. Lanercost, St Augustine's, Furness, Glastonbury and Whitby Abbeys are among the many destroyed and left to moulder on the destructive orders of Henry VIII, ruins of a monastic way of life that was holy, erudite, powerful and at times rich and corrupt. It was with a sense of awe that in Canterbury I saw the burial place of Augustine, who founded the Abbey in 598 and became the very first Archbishop of Canterbury. This ruin and the nearby church of St Martin (built before 597 and still in use) really deserve acknowledgement as the birthplace of Christianity in England.

Then the Cathedrals: Canterbury, Winchester, Salisbury, York, Leicester were the English ones I visited. But there had also been Chartres, Reims, Salzberg, Budapest, Krakow, Warsaw and others. What men could do with stone a thousand years ago is still miraculous – the technical wizardry, the artistry, the vision, the will to worship and reach heavenwards. To be where countless generations have prayed is still a powerful experience, and the soaring roofs, exquisite stained glass windows and spots like the worn centre of the Labyrinth in Chartres have a power that transports one into prayer.

Even more moving in some ways are the little stone parish churches, some with their narrow arched Norman windows, others with their later gothic points. While many have had multiple renovations over the centuries, they have often retained their original stone baptismal fonts from maybe the 8th or 9th centuries. To see these places where unnumbered ordinary souls began their journey of faith gave me a sense of connectedness to all who have gone before. And in England a surprising sense of 'them' having taken what was once 'ours'!

Maintaining these precious buildings large and small, great and humble has become a huge challenge for the Church of England as congregations have dwindled and government funding is not available. One little parish church has an active congregation of 28 and now needs a new roof. The cathedrals are beginning to charge admission as distinct from inviting donations – their maintenance bills can be £7000 or more a day. So these old stone buildings are both treasure and liability. The parish of Malton in Yorkshire found a creative solution: it gifted (some would say gifted back!) the church of St Leonard to the Catholic community. It is now one of the few churches its age in Catholic care.

Flying buttresses, carved statues of saints, kings and angels, reliefs of gospel scenes, delicate stone traceries inspire admiration for the masons who spent their lives designing and crafting these places of worship in honour of their God and His Blessed Mother. Intriguing, though, to find maverick pagan images of the old religion here and there in these most Christian of contexts: the green men, the sheela na gigs, the imp high on the pillar in Lincoln Cathedral, and the delicious face-pulling gargoyles of Canterbury

Cathedral. Were they part of the authorised design, or did the masons 'sneak' them in to make a point?

Then there are the sacred stones which mark the lives and deaths of individuals, the great and the insignificant. Being in Westminster Abbey moved me to tears, such was the presence of all that human greatness, the poets, the saints, the kings and queens, the reformers and politicians. But the sacred stones that had the biggest impact of all were those connected with my own ancestors.

Being invited in for a cuppa in a humble cottage in south-west Scotland which was my great-great-grandparents' home in the 1860s and 70s was an extraordinary experience – I'd only asked to take a photo! Tadcaster cemetery is the burial places of two sets of great-grandparents – one lot well enough off to have a sizable monument, the others unmarked, and not even together, as she was a Catholic and he wasn't! Acting on a hunch, I found a gravestone in Ripponden, another Yorkshire village, where another set of great-greats almost came out to meet me.

Through an 1898 newspaper clipping I knew that Frederick Rayner, a great-x 3 grandfather, had been one of the first teachers at the Leeds Parish National School, so went to see whether it still existed. The building itself has totally disappeared, but behind the Leeds Parish Church (St Peter's) there remains an enormously satisfying archway and wall with an inlaid foundation stone inscribed with Anno D(omini) MLCCCXII. So Frederick was beginning to instill learning into the little lads of Leeds while Napoleon was invading Russia!

Stones for millennia have been the material of choice for marking sacred spaces. Already when they were selected, shaped, installed they were millions of years old, formed by mighty pressures before humans walked the earth. Over the months I did a lot of touching and stroking of these various stones, aware of their great age and the paradox of my own insignificance. No wonder stones put us in touch with the Permanent, the Transcendent, the Source. No wonder St Peter, the Rock, recognised the words of Ps 118 and Isaiah as applying to Jesus:

It was the stone rejected by the builders that proved to be the keystone. Ps 118.22

Yahweh says this: See how I lay in Zion a stone of witness, a precious cornerstone, a foundation stone. The believer shall not stumble. And I will make justice the measure, integrity the plumb-line. Isaiah 28, 16-17

1996

Impressions of Poland

It was my travelling companion's idea to include Poland in our itinerary, but once the seed was sown the connections began to emerge for me until the lure was strong. There was the memory of listening to the Warsaw concerto on the radio as a small child as my mother explained that The War started when Hitler invaded Poland. Some knowing from those years that there had been a Polish army based in England, and that all Poles were Catholics. Kids at school in New Zealand with names that looked nothing like they sounded.

I'd never imagined ranging this far afield, but a venturesome companion made the trip possible. And what an enriching and tortured visit it was! We'd found ourselves on a Jewish path several countries earlier.

My friend, one of the Polish orphans who came to Pahiatua. The papal connection. The Solidarity saga of the eighties. The eventual freedom from communist domination. Closest of all the story of my foster-daughter's father, Tadeusz, removed, aged 17, by the invaders from his home in southern Poland in 1939, his war spent in a German labour camp, already an ill and broken man on his post-war arrival in New Zealand, and the ongoing repercussions of this experience for him and his family.

So yes, the chance of a lifetime to visit a land that in New Zealand and even European terms is 'a bit out of town'. We would be travelling by rental car from Budapest, through the Slovak Republic, to southern Poland to spend the first two nights in Krakow. I was relieved not to be involved in the driving, as we'd heard dire tales of Polish roads and drivers. First impressions over the border were of descending the High Tatra Mountains, then fenceless green plains and large well-kept houses. It looked prosperous. I wondered where Tadeusz had lived. It was not long before we saw men and women working in the fields with scythes and sickles, and hand-sowing seed – a glimpse of an ancient way of life. And cows, ropes tied around their horns, the other end attached to a tree, or being led across the road to a new patch of grass. Motorway signs alerted us to the possibility of horsedrawn carts, which duly appeared on a regular basis.

Krakow is justifiably famous: it was the old royal capital until 1596, and still understands itself as a spiritual capital. Its stunningly huge and beautiful Market Square is the largest medieval one in Europe. Its buildings have a definite exotic flavour. Krakow is the only city to have survived the war relatively untouched, as the Russians arrived in 1945 and forced a German withdrawal. Two mornings in a row we breakfasted under umbrellas on the perimeter of the Square as we watched the heart of Krakow waking up in the sun. Vans of fruit, vegetables, flowers, alcohol and bread, arriving to re-stock the restaurants, sellers of balloons and souvenirs setting up their stalls, live musicians. A delightful waitress who couldn't stop laughing at the strange New Zealand custom of having toast *underneath* the scrambled eggs – much sign language and disbelief! Wondered though about the number of folk with plastered wrists until it dawned that the uneven footpaths were the likely culprits! And it seemed that the civic structures don't do much street-cleaning: people were out sweeping and scrubbing their own bit of footpath themselves.

Off the negative end on the pleasure scale was the pilgrimage to Auschwitz, Oswiecim, as it appears on the map. Even the prior knowings did not cushion the horror of the reality. I found it impossible to take photos or buy postcards, and was appalled by the sight of 8-10 year olds there on a school visit, despite a notice that under 14s would not be admitted. To tell the details to possibly unwilling hearers would itself be a violence. The spirits of Anne Frank and Maximilian Kolbe linger on along with all the other millions. 'Why did you go there?' asked a friend once I was back. I've wrestled for an answer, and the nearest I can get is 'the willingness to pay the cost of knowing'. And somewhere in that the legend of the knight Parsifal who healed the wound of the Fisher King when he learned to ask the question 'What are you going through?' It took a few days to begin recovering from the experience. Then off to Warsaw, 320k to the north, to do some more seeing for ourselves. 'Seeing' was the operative word because despite the cheerful predictions in the guide books little or no English was spoken. We were in a virtual linguistic vacuum for the five days of our visit – nothing said and little written told us anything: we were reliant on our senses and intuition, very aware that we could be misinterpreting anything and everything, and there was no way to check things out. A wonderful hostel room with huge feather pillows was a welcome contrast to the bleak room we'd had in Krakow. Warsaw seemed small and manageable after the size of Vienna and Budapest. We headed for the old town centre, where the 'medieval' buildings have all been restored in replica after the total devastation of World War II, when 80% of the city's buildings were razed, and 50% of its population killed. Imagine that in Wellington or Dunedin! Whatever else the communist regime stifled, it apparently didn't get in the way of this extraordinary restoration project which was completed by the late 1950s.

The war is still very much in evidence nonetheless. Postcards with 'then and now' shots of ruin and resurrection. Churches with plaques, memorials, candles, flowers. A Christ crucified in prison garb on a gallows-tree in memory of the Katyn Woods massacre. The memorial square that was the ghetto. The razed site of the Secret Police Headquarters with its trees, one dead, one green and growing. The names, the names, the names.... A city still seemingly suffering from post-traumatic stress. 'How', we wanted to ask, 'do you live with all this?' The full churches must be part of the answer, churches where there might be a mass, confessions, adoration of the Blessed Sacrament all going on at once in different areas. The freedom to worship again, and the portraits of the favourite son. Each town seems to have its ulica Jana Pawla II (John Paul II Street).

A surprising glimpse of home: in the City Historical Museum in the main square, again doing the hard work of looking and seeing the evidence of the hell years, we came across an inscription joltingly in English as well as Polish. It told us that the photograph of Stefan Starzynski, Mayor of Warsaw in 1939, and eventually killed by the Nazis, had been presented by the Polish Community of Wellington, New Zealand! Who had put it in their suitcase to take to the other side of the world? And who sent it back? Just hearing a couple speaking English was enough for us to celebrate this connection with them!

And a pilgrimage to the suburban church of St Stanislaw Kostka, last base and tomb of Father Jerzy Popieluszko, who after four years chaplaincy to striking steel workers, was kidnapped and murdered by the secret police in October 1984. This was in the early days of the Solidarity movement which had such a huge impact on the struggle for a free Poland. He had instigated adult education for them based on Gospel justice, Church social justice teachings, law, economics, and negotiation techniques. His body was discovered in the Vistula River ten days later. The funeral at his own church was attended by an estimated four hundred thousand Poles. He is honoured as a martyr. Even as we visited, two bus loads of pilgrims arrived to pray at his tomb and in his church. It is fair to say that his death was a major catalyst for an even more pugnacious push for a free Poland. Solidarity re-emerged. Communism crumbled.

All this was the lens through which we watched the celebrations for Children's Day on the first Sunday in June, again from under a café umbrella. It was hot! Hundreds of families were there cherishing their children, giving them treats, there as here with balloons, ice-creams, puppet shows, rides in horse-drawn carriages. Smiles and happiness and the hope for the future of Poland! But underneath were the grandparents remembering how it was when they were that size? And hoping all that will not happen again? That same afternoon we watched a cheerful demonstration urging support for joining the European Union in the forthcoming referendum. The 'Tak' (yes) on the placards was in our minute Polish vocabulary. They blew whistles, banged drums, handed out leaflets. Again we had un-askable questions and no-one to ask: how will this help you? What will happen to your rural population if they are hurled too quickly into the 21st century?

Then the 340k drive south-west to Wroclaw (pronounced, as far as we could figure, Vrotswafl!). It had been chosen as a convenient way-station between Warsaw and Prague, but turned out to be a delightful interlude in its own right. The river winds around the famous old university city, and a multiplicity of churches, some very old, appear about one per block. One held the tomb of Renaissance scholar Erasmus. Another was St Mary Magdalene's where, unusually, the patron saint appears on the altar backing – courtesy of a Calvary scene in which she figures. During our 'church crawl' we accidentally found ourselves in the Archbishop's vege garden. And were politely but firmly pointed to the way out. Wroclaw, visually anyway, is less haunted by the war. And loads of well-dressed young people were doing the café and study life. It too has a wonderful huge market square surrounded by colourful building facades, where we had some pierogi, special little Polish cheese and potato dumplings. Another notable meal along the way was a cold beetroot soup with chopped vegetables and hard boiled eggs.

And so on to the Czech border after a memorable five days, and after considerable practice in mime and drawing to explain our needs! Phrase books can only do so much: try asking for a plug for the basin in your room, or explaining what a shandy is in Polish. A picture is worth a thousand words! Consideration then of the tourist/colonial idea that 'they' should speak 'our' language, and knowing it to be untrue, but relief when even basic communication was accomplished. 'Hello' (dzien dobry), 'please' (proscze), and 'thank you' (dziekuje) was as far as we got with Polish!

Poland is passionate, and overt about it. Poland elicits profound emotional reactions in response. Admiration for the beauty, horror at what it has had to endure, awe at the Resurrection faith and the sustained and costly fight for freedom, hope for its on-going development. May God continue to heal its past wounds and bless its future!

2003

A Stone

'Bring a stone for the altar at Myrtos'
Pragmatic – case heavy already
Beach find – ah, pumice, light!

Then it told me its story:
Rock heart to the mountain
Molten by fire from deeper belly
Hurled skywards boiling bubbling
Globule falling cooling
Water-borne stream river sea

Earth fire air water
Seeing my story too
Solidity meltdown
Flung by force to another dimension
Lighter now
Air permeated
And so I float

2006

> A major adventure, a
> Goddess Pilgrimage
> to Crete, was
> imminent. We were
> asked to bring a stone
> from home.

A Goddess Pilgrimage in Crete

> A most
> extraordinary
> two weeks. And
> some enduring
> and fruitful
> friendships.

The leaflet for this drew me like a magnet when author and thealogian Carol Christ spoke at Massey University in February 2005. It may as well have been a pilgrimage to Mars! A year later I realised sales of my first book could make it a real possibility. My application for a scholarship was well received – useful having a track record of writing for and working with women on their lives and spirituality! Useful too that our five Wellington weekends of women's workshops had been called Womenspirit Rising, named for Carol's 1979 book. There were many amazing experiences during the two weeks, and multiple fascinating archaeological sites and museums, swims in warm turquoise waters, tavernas with wonderful food. These diary extracts from days that were more intense than others pick up the main themes that emerged for me there: being with women, both other pilgrims and local women, as we shared our stories and experienced life and spirituality together; deep encounters, some literally so, with the Divine as Goddess, Mother Earth; a challenging theological reflection that initially shocked me, and still isn't really sorted; and learning the human history of this long-inhabited island. And then there is my ongoing connection with the San Francisco women, and visits in both directions – all that lay in the future.

Setting out

The first evening we gathered on the hotel roof. Three from Canada, two Kiwis and the rest from USA. Two ordained ministers, a Lutheran who runs a feminist parish, and an Episcopalian who has worked towards a bicultural parish with Native Americans. A significant number with a Catholic background, mostly in their youth. A similar number with a Lutheran background. Most thought of themselves as Christian. A few from a wiccan or astrology background, and one adamantly disowning all labels. In age we ranged from 32 to 69. Karolina (Carol uses the Greek version of her name during the pilgrimages) and her assistant Christina welcomed us, and introduced the ritual for the times we'd gather: each of us was to say 'I am whole, I am here, I am (name)' and the circle would repeat this back. A powerful affirmation! Then we named our maternal lines. I enjoyed being able to say 'I am Trish, daughter of Freda, daughter of Sarah Jane, daughter of Annie Elizabeth, daughter of Isabella'. That is the fruit of my genealogy research, and connects my family back to the early 1800s. So far nothing different from what we've done in women's groups at home.

Our first ancient site was Knossos. I'd learned something about it at school, never dreaming that I'd ever get there! We learned about the layers of Cretan civilisations, and the catastrophic earthquakes that at intervals levelled the complex buildings, serially rebuilt on the same sites until, presumably discouraged, the population deserted them. They were covered with the silt of time for 2500 to 3000 years. It was only in the early 20th century that teams of archaeologists from various countries descended on Crete, dug, and were astounded by what they discovered. From the Minoan period which was our focus, there were statues of Her in various manifestations (snake goddess, bird goddess), well-crafted jewellery in gold, huge two metre high decorated storage pots for oil and grain and much more.

So there we were in this awesome place, the heat shimmering over the baked ground, the huge building as Evans reconstructed it in the early 1900s over the original ruins. Someone had apparently complained about Karolina's tour groups doing rituals in archaeological sites, so such activities had been banned. Nonetheless we walked silently in single file along the main pathway into the building, and later round other areas. A powerful acknowledgement that this was a place where the Goddess had been honoured, and her priestesses had tended her rituals!

The Mary Issue

Each morning on the bus we were invited to join in our daily morning prayer to help us focus on the quest we were on together. As we travelled on day 2, we were invited to choose a ribbon from a small fabric bag without looking, and to see what it said to us. Mine turned out to be a blah beige – the last colour I'd have chosen, given any choice. It said absolutely nothing to me until I held it up to show Cathy, and I noticed it was an exact match for the parched earth outside. There had been no rain for three or four months. Another ribbon bag went round – this time to find the matching ribbon. That made two blah beige ribbons!

We were on our way to the mountain convent of Paliani, which was called 'old' in the 6th century AD. There were some tiny cheerful black-swathed nuns who had individual homes around the perimeter of the enclosure. In the centre was a whitewashed church, behind which was their ancient sacred myrtle tree, itself several hundred years old. Hung from its gnarled and tangled branches are many metal thanksgiving tokens from grateful pray-ers, and beside it a heap of no-longer-needed crutches. We gathered under the tree to hear Karolina and one of the sisters chant its legend in Greek: a wonder-working icon of Mary was miraculously found in the tree when the church had burned down, was retrieved and restored to the new church, but had 'escaped' back to the tree a few more times. And there she is still!

We encircled the tree, and pondered what we'd say about our colour when we'd tie on our ribbon to form a prayer intention for ourselves. I knew that my own intention for the whole pilgrimage was for the release of tears – it is years since I've had a good cry. And then the jolt: what I had to say about my ribbon was that it was the colour of dry land waiting for the rains! An ohmyGoddess moment! So we left our ribbons and intentions in the care of the tree – or was it of Mary? or the Goddess? Then into their beautiful little church, highly ornate, festooned with chandeliers and icons. I could not bring myself to kiss the Mary image as most of the others were doing, reverently following Karolina's example. Were they calling her Goddess??!

Post Vatican II Catholics have deconstructed the image of Mary as the feminine face of God. And there have been the centuries of accusations that Catholics worship Mary. I can't even begin thinking of her as Goddess! She's human like us! In Greece, Mary is known as Panagia – literally the All Holy One.

In the refectory the nuns gave us homemade bread and potent Greek coffee in little cups. The one young one (early 20s) told us about her life, and her faith that God would provide for the convent, and not let it die out. As the average age of the others seemed to be about eighty, the risk is real! The one who had sung the tree's story earlier told us she had wanted to become a nun as a 12 year-old and her parents had reluctantly allowed this. A delightful visit!

Back on the bus we had a wonderful surprise. Stacy, the Lutheran pastor, had developed a feminist rosary. She gave each of us a set of rosary beads she'd made. All beautiful, with four 'decades' of seven beads separated by larger ones. Mine are stunning. The decade beads are carnelians and pale rose quartz separated by tiny pearls. The larger beads have cloisonné'd pink flowers on an earth-red background. Instead of a crucifix there is a beautiful little swirling figure which could be Goddess, or a breaking wave, or... The prayers came with them.

I love Catholic Sister Miriam Therese Winter's:

> Our Mother, who is within us, we celebrate your many names.
> Your wisdom come, your will be done unfolding from the depths within us.
> Each day you give us all that we need.
> You remind us of our limits and we let go.
> You support us in our power and we act with courage.
> For you are the dwelling-place around us,
> The empowerment within us,
> And the celebration among us.
> Now and forever. Amen.

I had more difficulty with the adaptation of Karolina's prayer which in turn adapted the Hail Mary:

> Hail Goddess, full of grace, blessed are you
> And blessed are all the fruits of your womb.
> For you are the Mother of us all.
> Hear us now and in all our needs.
> O blessed be, O blessed be. Amen

It was too hard to separate addressing Goddess from the traditional Hail Mary prayer. I couldn't figure out who I was talking to, the human Mary or the feminine image of the Divine/ Goddess! For Karolina they did seem to be the same.

Death, then and now

I'd offered to help with the next day's ritual, knowing only that it was about death. As I read the book, I realised how complex and deep it was going to be. And so it was. We walked a long way through an arid plantation of olive trees. Eventually there was the Minoan thalos – a circular stone tomb perhaps four metres in diameter, now minus its roof, with a low arched entrance. Outside were the walls of what had been ossuaries, small rooms where the bones had been stored communally after decomposition in the main area. It was used 4000-4500 years ago.

We lined up crone-ologically, the eldest at the head of the line. My towel was laid under the low, low entrance to the tomb, and Cindy and I began the ritual questioning of those who came. She asked 'Have you tasted the seed of death?' And I asked 'Are you willing to learn the mystery?' Only those who answered yes to the second question were invited to enter the tomb. All did. Then we asked each other, and we too got down on hands and knees – became 'humble' 'close to the earth' to enter the tomb. Once inside we put our special things on the low rock that was our altar: seeds, flowers, little Goddess figures.

One by one we named our dead, and poured our libations of milk, oil, honey or wine over the altar. It was good for me to name the two dear friends who had died since I'd left home for this trip, and whose funerals I'd been so sad to miss. And my husband and mother. For many it was a very emotional time. Then Cindy and I offered a communion. She had a jar of nuts in honey, and fed one to each woman saying 'Taste the seed of life' and I had a goblet of wine to offer: 'Receive the wine of regeneration'. It was a powerful experience, and was a blessed opportunity for me to again minister in that way as I had during all my years as minister of the Eucharist.

A Village

After breakfast I was startled by Maggie doing healing touch on someone's shoulder, and turning away to shake her hands. It was the self-same gesture used by the Kalahari tribes-people in the video seen at the course at uni last year, and by us at prayer group in the 70s and 80s! Asked her where she had learned it – but no real answer – I told her why I asked, and she suggested it simply came from the collective unconscious.

Three of us went down to the village of Zaros. Much going on: the fish truck with its boxes of ice on an open tray, a massive truck sidling round corners to deliver flour to the bakers, men sunning themselves and flicking their beads, women working in shops or invisible at home. One worked her loom in the open shop frontage, and we stopped to watch and buy. I chose two little cloths, one for myself, and the other as my gift for the last evening of the tour. It seemed that 'small' and 'packable' were good criteria!

Religious icons were everywhere – including in the bank. Then a café. The elderly owner squeezed oranges for our juice – a drink fit for the Goddess! I'd looked at the family photos on the walls, dating back to at least the 1950s, and recognised a much younger version of our hostess. So when she'd brought the drinks, I took her over and without a word of common tongue, I was told about her siblings, daughter and grand-daughter as they took part in family festivals and village life. She then brought us a gift of cake. Good to have contact with ordinary women!

Back at the hotel I chatted to a German woman, part of a tour group and curious about what our group was doing together. I told her 'spiritual things'. 'Not scientology?' she asked dubiously. 'No, not that, sharing our lives and stories as we travel.' 'Ah!' Comprehension! So she explained she helps organise the World Day of Prayer which is marked in many countries in early March. She had visited Paraguay where the 2007 service was being prepared.

Height and Depth

The most intense day of the whole trip! A couple of hours drive to Mt Juctas, then we packed like sardines into a small bus, and lurched up a track. A little below one of the peaks of this two-breasted mountain we piled out to clamber to the top. There were the remains of a Minoan peak shrine – back then as now the tops of mountains had a sacred role. On the other peak is a little white chapel dedicated to the Transfiguration of Jesus.

There was a deep, deep cleft in the rock into which people all those millennia ago dropped prayer tokens. I was more entranced by exquisite crocus-like yellow flowers which somehow managed to find enough sustenance to bloom on those arid heights. They seemed to have absorbed the colour of sunlight. I lay face down on a slanting slab of rock, sun warmed despite the height. My eyes closed, and I had a deep sense of being held and supported by Mother Earth/the Goddess. Could have stayed there a long time! A wonderful vista stretched way below, olive groves, vines, a few villages right out to the sea. And above us wheeled and glided half a dozen griffin buzzards. A ballet in slow, slow motion! Definitely a 'peak experience'!

Then back down and to the little village of Skoteino. Karolina has an arrangement which benefits everyone: two local women provide lunch for her tour groups twice a year. Christina and Marika had made us a wonderful banquet of stuffed tomatoes, ditto vine leaves, moussaka, salads and cheese pie. Much pleasure, much appreciation and much left over!

A trip into the Skoteino Cave. We donned headlights, and received candles as well. Then down… and down… and down… On the second level down we used a rock shelf as an altar to place the goddess figures, my little Athena owl and candles, and poured our libations. Close by was a deep hole between the rocks. We'd been asked to bring a symbol of something in our lives that we wanted to let go. Then one by one we threw it down the hole saying 'I am naked, I am letting go, I am leaving behind ….' I wanted to throw away my wing feathers to be more earthed, and my childhood vow that I would never again let anyone make me cry. My symbol was a strong wing feather that did not want to go down the hole – it took three attempts. I was moved by the others' leavings – fears, low self-esteem, and one left her powers there and threw in her candle. It was a healing, sacramental ritual.

Most of us continued on down, helped through the tricky bits by a couple of men with ropes. Eventually, just us, we were down four levels in a womb room deep in the belly of the earth. The two women who caught me as I slithered round the last narrow bent passage felt like midwives. We settled in this deep place, turned out our lights and sat in silence and darkness for a long time. Whoever first needed to was to say 'Let there be light', and the candles would be relit. No-one did. Whether one's eyes were open or shut, the darkness was the same. I loved it – the most intense darkness I've ever been in. And so it seemed did the others, though I heard later of terrors of spiders and other crawlies. Eventually Karolina initiated the relighting with her candle, and as we passed light from one to the other, there was for me the obvious parallel with the Easter vigil.

The guides helped us back up the tricky bits, and there were ladders for climbing where we'd slid down on our rears. We helped each other, rejoined those who'd stayed further up, and headed to the light. Some were exhausted and had pushed through their limits. I was exhilarated, tired, and relieved that the whole thing had been so much easier than Lost World, the caving expedition described in *Faith Evolving*.

We emerged filthy with the reddish mud of the cave, and changed some gear before getting back on the bus. Back to Christina and Marika to make inroads into the left-overs! They wanted to know about our lives and tell us about theirs. Listening to the stories, I realised that those with children were in a minority. Unsurprisingly, I with my 6+1 children and squad of grandchildren had the most. Marika, now 80, married at 19, has a 96 year-old husband and they get on very well. She told us how she'd loved school, but when she was 12 'the Germans came' – end of formal education! She was delighted that her children and grandchildren had done more. But when they have been to university in Athens, the young ones are reluctant to return as employment opportunities are limited. It was lovely to have contact with local women, and I was moved by how hard their lives had been compared with mine.

On to the tourist centre of Agios Nikolaos where the hotel had upgraded us. What luxury lay in wait! Cathy and I were allocated a 5th floor room, with a view of the harbour across the road. All incredibly beautiful! And a bath! Given the exertions of the day, we couldn't wait to soak first ourselves, then our cave clothes. It was soon dark and a full orange moon rose dramatically over the harbour. Several of us went for a swim. Just so warm and lovely! What height and depths we'd had that day! Then the black and moonlit sea! A poem began to germinate. See *Going Back* p.83.

Relics, Birthing and Reflection

Malia was the next archaeological sacred site, smaller than Knossos, with better facilities. I loved the gigantic jars, restored jigsaw-like after their demise in an earthquake probably 3500 years ago. As Marija Gimbutas describes in her major work *The Language of the Goddess*[24], they were decorated with spirals and waves, snakes, feathers, circles.

Then to the cave of Eilethia, the goddess of childbirth, and honoured here from Neolithic times till about 700 CE. A short scramble down into the cave, then near its entrance was an omphalos stone, a round boulder with a 'navel' in the middle, geologically an incipient stalagmite and mythically a pregnant belly. Untold generations of pregnant women have laid their bellies against it to ask for a blessing. Inside was a group of stalagmites resembling a mother and children. And beyond, a couple of small sacred pools, where we followed the ancient practice of blessing ourselves and our womanhood with the water. A very feminine place! The Divine One was powerfully with us.

I was surprised at our evening circle at what I said about the previous day's infant experiences. Yes, the mountain top experience had been like lying at a breast, fully supported. The slither down into the cave had felt like a birth-canal, but I hadn't till that moment connected the swim with being re-immersed in the uterine waters of the Earth Mother. We said Stacy's Goddess rosary. I'd been looking forward to using my beautiful beads. Praying 'Our Mother' was very right, 'Hail Goddess' was confusing. The words absorbed from my earliest childhood still could not be detached from the original addressee, and I simply couldn't conceive of Mary as Goddess. And the sensation of beads-through-fingers took me back to a place I'd happily left behind. I will find a new way to use this beautiful gift!

More Mary, More Caves

On to the village of Platanos to the church of St Mary in Chains, where there is another 'travelling' icon. It was three times captured and taken to Constantinople, and three times miraculously returned, the last time complete with the chains and column intended to restrain it! I asked Karolina for a conversation about Mary at some stage, and she said 'Let's start now'. So sitting outside, looking across the valley, I explained my dilemma, and asked what she did with Mary's virginity. 'Oh,' she said rather airily, 'I just ignore it!' For a cradle Catholic, that position is simply not possible! And then, 'Take what fits and leave the rest'. That's how it will have to be!

A cave on Mt Dictys was the most touristy of all. I was glad of the 300 steps and hand-rail, but could have passed on the electric lighting. Soon we and hordes of others were down to the bottom. Incredible formations, stalagmites and stalactites that had united aeons ago – waterfalls, trees, organ pipes, rippling curtains all in stone. A sacred place, and I was saddened at what seemed like desecration – the beautiful pool littered with coins from visitors. I'd have loved more time there – in solitude and silence. This is one of two caves claimed to be where Rhea gave birth to baby Zeus.

More appealing was the darkness of our next cave, Trapeza, where we sat in a circle with our candles, and sang a song of affirmation to each one by name. Lovely to both give and receive! Even more powerful for me was naming the women who have mentored, taught and encouraged us. My four are forever taonga (treasures) in my life. And I remembered as well the New Zealand men who had fought and died on this island during WWII.

Recognitions

At the next museum I took a very deep breath when I saw a collection of little clay women, almost identical to those I'd made in 2004, but from about 4000 years ago! I shared that story at circle time. A British woman archaeologist asked whether that's what we were too. I said our tour had a spiritual purpose, exploring the Goddess culture of the Minoans. She was from Celtic Cornwall, and when I described Karolina's understanding that Knossos etc were sacred sites rather than palaces, her eyes widened and she said 'Yes, I could just about hear their skirts rustling there'.

In a 14th century church, we saw frescoes, mainly of Mary's life, their colours still fresh and bright. The final painting was a painfully eloquent depiction of the shift to patriarchal religion: at the Last Judgement, Father God is demanding that Mother Earth give up the bodies of her children to be judged, and there she is with crown and snake, having no option but to comply. After that it was a bit of light relief to wander round the stalls of jewellery, weavings and icons.

Next stop the Gournia village excavations, which really moved me. They stretched up a slope, a Minoan Coronation Street, ordinary homes of ordinary people, the remnants of their daily life still there in the grinding stones and storage rooms. We walked their paved pathways from 4000 to 3500 years ago. I felt them there still. This area was excavated by US-trained Harriet Boyd in the early 1900s. The male archaeologists would not let her join their digs, so she hired a team of locals and did her own!

Through mountains along the northern coast, then down a goat-track to the tiny fishing village of Mochlos. Our circle gathered in the court-yard under a vine-draped 'roof' heavy with bunches of fat pink grapes. Then we dined beside the sea. Delicious local fish, and figs... oh the figs! Green, smaller than the purple ones we'd had earlier, barely more than a mouthful, and they were heaven! I was startled by Maggie's telling me of her reaction to seeing me at breakfast our first morning in Heraklion. She said she'd seen a white light around me, and wondered 'Who is that woman? She's a white witch, a healer.' And I'd been just having my muesli and chatting to the others! Felt very honoured.

The Island Day

Then a gem of a rest day! Stillness and quiet needed first. Later with four others I swam to the little island where there is an archaeological site. It was only 200-300 metres so quite feasible. The others pushed an inflatable mattress over with their gear on it. I'd opted for only what I was wearing: togs, wet shoes, and t-shirt. It was an amazing sensation to clamber ashore on the island having got there by our own efforts. Very primal!

There immediately were ruined stone walls of houses built in layers, after the serial earthquake devastations. Probably some Neolithic traces, much Minoan work, and later layers through to Byzantine times. And a little white chapel. We climbed carefully over the ancient walls to explore. Higher up there were many shards of pottery, loose or sticking out of the bank, just begging for some careful digging. I picked up a 12cm fragment of hollow pipe. Who made it? Who last held it? Was it a musical instrument or a spout from a vessel? After holding my questions, knowing the answers were lost in time, I laid it gently back beside the path. No-one would have known if I'd taken it home… but even the touching seemed somewhat sacrilegious, as did walking on the old ruined walls. Despite our utmost reverence!

We'd been told to look out for the red triangle shaped stone at the lintel of a probable sacred pool for women. And there it was, gleaming in the sun. Surely a tribute to the sacred generative power of women, so honoured in those days! I wandered further round to see the rock cave tombs, then as there was still a decent swim between me and lunch, I decided to head off back on my own. We'd been told to do it alone only if we were strong swimmers. I had a happy solo journey, and it was so satisfying to do the expedition simply with my own resources!

At dusk we processed single file and snake-like a few hundred metres along the coast for our labyrinth ritual. It was very different from my previous labyrinth encounters. The contour was different, a more mushroom-shaped version, rather than the round Chartres one. And whereas I'd known it previously as a solitary meditative journey where passing opposing traffic could be tricky, this time was intentionally communal. Encounters with those near us were with eye and hand contact, and we did a two-handed greeting with a ceremonial twirl when there was a need to pass someone going the other way. This added a whole new dimension to what is frequently a deep experience.

After a spiral dance on the nearby ancient threshing floor, we stood in a circle and sang a Native American chant to Grandmother Moon. And there she was, floating just a little less fully above us.

Altar, Poems and Rain
We headed south across the island to Myrtos, closest point to Africa, and stopped on the main coast road. There was a challenging high greasy bank to climb. By now we had a good routine of the fitter, more agile ones helping those who wanted a hand. This time I was happy to both give and receive. We were visiting an Early Minoan site, the traces of houses where there had been loom weights found – evidence of weaving from 2500-2000 BCE, and the statue of a 'turtle-necked' goddess figure. We'd been asked to bring a stone from home for the altar at Myrtos.

I had chosen a piece of pumice from Waikanae Beach, probably from the cataclysmic Taupo eruption in 186 CE. It had told me its story which became a poem (p67). A flat stone was our altar, where we put several goddess figures, Stacy's gift rosaries and other precious things. We each spoke of our stones. One that touched me came with the greetings of a husband 'and all men who support your search for the Divine Feminine'. He had given his wife this pilgrimage as a 25th wedding anniversary present!! I told my stone's story and laid it carefully on the altar. And immediately its larger 'pores' became a face. Again we poured libations, acknowledging the sacredness of what we had just done together.

Back north to the Dictean Mountains. Along the way we each chose a poem of Sappho's to read at Aphrodite's shrine above Kato Symi. Near a beautiful spring, we stood in a circle round a little altar and read our poems. This was sadly interrupted when a wasp, one of many, flew up a woman's trouser leg and stung her. The mood of connection with the past was broken for me by the need to be vigilant in the present! If there'd been lots of wasps up on the hillside, when we'd rattled down for our goat stew lunch at the local taverna there was a positive plague. I found the Americans' insistence that the wasps were 'bees' and that they 'bit' somewhat disconcerting. We Kiwis had already discerned that we were linguistic foreigners, even if we all thought we were speaking English!

Later the rain started – torrentially! We'd been lucky with the weather for travelling, but the country was so parched and thirsty, it seemed a cause for celebration. I found myself chanting, mostly in my head, 'And the rains came to water the earth'. And wondering whether this was the precursor to my own drought breaking!

More Women's Stories
Next morning the rain cleared for our visit to an archaeological site in the midst of a current village where people have built homes for at least 4000 years. We explored the remains of two or three very large houses, with ornamental paving still in good repair. Then visited three generations of women who sell their weavings. Maria, the mother in her 60s, supplied us with strong coffee made a cup at a time over the little gas burner in her kitchen. Daughter Stella in her 40s, has a son, an Elvis-looking pop idol. We saw posters of him back in Heraklion. And a daughter at university in Athens. The grandmother, a minute frail 90 year-old, told us of her tragic life. She hadn't married until she was 40. Her husband was brain-damaged while trying to escape the opposing forces in the civil war after WWII. He'd stayed under water too long while hiding from his hunters. Then their only son had been killed in an accident. She had subsequently adopted a son, her 'soul child', who married Maria whom she had trained in the weaving and the business. These old ones have had hard, hard lives!

Our last cave, on Mt Ida, was the other reputed site of the birth of Zeus, also with a shelf on which the delivery was said to have occurred. It was freezing up there despite polyprops and parka, strange after the heat, and there'd been a challenging ride up on the jam-packed back of a ute... well out of my comfort zone! After thawing and eating by the taverna's big wood fire, we crawled down the mountain in the bus, with visibility at times virtually nil, past fractured rocks, with rain sheeting off them. The streambeds, bone-dry yesterday, began to fill as the water found its way down the mountain. We were told of the late summer greening that would follow within a couple of days. It seemed a wonderful metaphor for my life now!

Parting and Pondering

Our time together closed with a final circle. Again we each affirmed 'I am whole, I am here, I am (Trish)'. Then I led the naming prayer: 'What are your special names for Goddess? Now listen for Her special name for you'. I heard later of at least a couple who had powerful experiences. We chose a gift from the bag and read out its message. Marie got my little cloth, with its words about its origin with the weaver in Zaros, about women having worked and played with threads since forever, and our having been woven into a good fabric in our time together. I received a little spoon with the beautiful 'two bees' design on the end. We sang again to Grandmother Moon, then walked to our farewell dinner. Tomorrow we go our separate ways, much enriched by the amazing potpourri of experiences of the last two weeks.

Karolina had defined 'pilgrimage' at the outset as being a journey with spiritual intent, ideally communal, taking us outside our comfort zones, with the journey being as important as the destination(s). With all that in mind, it has been pilgrimage indeed! Many deep and moving moments, in the company of my new sisters, some stretching times too. The times 'between' as important as those at specific sacred places. I appreciated all over again the life of privilege I have at home, compared with the lives of the women of Crete, particularly the older ones who lived through the war. It is an accident of geography that our islands are isolated and safe, while because of its strategic position theirs has had marauding armies tramping through it since forever. Some privilege can't be discarded, but it can be appreciated! And the Goddess? I felt her presence and breath at many moments. We found Her at Her shrines, as Mother Earth, in our rituals, in each other, in the local women we met and in ourselves. Is Mary Goddess? To say 'yes' to that will take a lot of exploring and pondering. For me for now they do not share an identity. To be continued…

Going Back

An awe-filled
Pilgrimage day.

Morning mountain breast
Embraced supported
I can relax
Is this my breath I feel
Or Hers?
Flower thriving in dry rock niche
Yellow like the sun
Buzzards gliding
Riding air

Sight gone
Eyes open eyes shut
Makes no difference
Born back into dark
Sliding bent through narrow way
Received by welcoming hands
Dark and pregnant silence
We know we are here
Alone together

Floating weightless
In the warmth
Of full-mooned silky sea
And tasting there
The salty uterine waters
That grew me to birth
I'm going back
To my Source
To Her

2006

Sacred Times in San Francisco

Another pilgrimage, this time to be at a conference organised by friends from Crete.

The Goddess Pilgrimage to Crete seemed so unlikely, yet it happened in 2006. A 2007 trip to San Francisco for a conference put on by women I'd met there also seemed so unlikely. But that too happened! It was an astonishingly rich and joyful experience, with both the expected and the unexpected. The conference was to be held at Ebenezer Lutheran Church[25], a suburban parish known as 'herchurch'. The dynamic pastor, Rev Stacy Boorn, wanted to celebrate the 20th anniversary of her ordination by convening a conference called *Wisdom's Urgent Cry* to look at the challenge to all Christian churches of feminine imagery for God.

I arrived several days ahead of the conference. The same day I was taken to a cathedral not made by human hands. Muir Woods, some miles out of the city, is a redwood forest. These majestic trees, some over 1000 years old and straight as the proverbial dies, are awe-inspiring. They too, like the spires of the stone cathedrals, reach skywards, and with their thick bark they can endure the fires that used to rage through the area. The air is fresh and cool as we exchange breath directly with these beautiful living things. When one dies or is badly damaged, the burls around the base of the trunk send out shoots which become daughter trees sharing the same root system. A wonderful symbol for community! Seeing, smelling, touching such ancient life was deeply moving. Simply to sit and absorb their peace, stability and endurance is prayer itself.

Mostly to remember my Franciscan tertiary mother-in-law, I visited Mission Dolores, the original mission station of the Franciscans in the area, and from which the city takes its name. This was founded in 1776, and the first mass had been celebrated there five days before the signing of the Declaration of Independence. Some of the original complex still exists 200 plus years later. The chapel, with its four foot thick adobe walls, was completed in 1796. It has a fascinating Indian patterned ceiling, and baroque Spanish altar and side-altars. Padre Junipero Serra, the founder of the mission, built it as part of a major complex, of which a model on display is an interesting overview.

Padre Junipero and his brothers developed a good relationship with the original Ohlone people of the area, and many of them became Christians. The chapel survived, some say miraculously, the 1906 earthquake and the citywide fire which followed it. The big church next door to it was bulldozed at that stage to clear a firebreak. The basilica now beside the chapel was built later. But to really experience the timelessness of this historic Mission, it is good to go into the little walled cemetery that has been there since the end of the 18th century. Roses and deep peace, the grave of Junipero himself, a great mix of English, Spanish, Irish, French names: Carr, Casanueva, Casey, Castillo, Cheminant, Cobb... And a beautiful small statue of Our Lady of the Mohawks, dressed in Indian clothes and standing on a plinth, is a memorial to 'Our Faithfull Indians'. I doubt whether the missionaries would have heard of inculturation, but they did it anyway!

Next on my list was the Episcopalian Grace Cathedral to visit their labyrinth. It is a French neo-Gothic stone structure on the brow of one of the city hills – and on a cable car route. It was built after the same 1906 quake, when two wealthy families donated the land on which their mansions had stood. These, along with much of the city, had been levelled in the disaster. I discovered not one labyrinth but two, modelled on that of the 12th century cathedral at Chartres near Paris. That in turn was the same shape as a 1st century Roman mosaic labyrinth I saw in the remains of a villa in Paphos, Cyprus after the Crete trip, which linked it to the mythic story of Thesus, Ariadne and the Minotaur in Crete. All more ancient than we knew!

The outside labyrinth at Grace was inlaid many years ago into the forecourt, but the permanent one inside behind the seating is a recent installation. Previously there was a carpet version that was unrolled there. A whole spirituality of labyrinth has emerged in recent years – as a meditation walk, as a mini-pilgrimage, as a metaphor for the journey within, as a way to seek solutions for difficulties. The surprises at Grace were the beautiful AIDS Memorial Chapel, the Bufano larger-than-life size statue of a benign St Francis, and the wonderful murals along the main walls. These depict the history of the church on that site, and the benefactors who enabled the building of this holy place.

For old times sake I visited St Mary's Cathedral, the inner-city contemporary Catholic Cathedral, consecrated in 1971. Its four smooth sails rise to a high square spire. It is affectionately known locally as the Whirlpool, a reference to a perceived likeness to a make of washing machine. From inside, the sails are seen to be connected by ladders of jewel-like stained glass, and to gaze upwards is to see them form a dramatic cross over the centre of the floor. The sweet sweep of space, the other glowing windows and the glorious waterfall of filament lights over the main altar are inspiring. It is a truly awesome house of God, contemporary, but simple and uncluttered. I can imagine it still being treasured by those who worship there in another 200 years!

The next event was a total surprise: Deborah who had been with us in Crete told me she was going to a Spiral Dance that evening, put on by Starhawk and her Reclaiming Community[26], and did I want to go too? I was enthralled by the prospect! This was the 28th such occasion, to mark the Feast of the Dead/Samhain/Harvest Festival/All Souls Day/death of the year. It was in a suburban gymnasium. We queued with a wonderful assortment of people, some like us in street clothes, others in a variety of medieval and mystical garb. San Francisco is truly the most inclusive place I've been to – and there were some in drag too, including an elderly man in a gorgeous purple ball-gown. We were in time to look at the altars around the hall's periphery, some of which I found very moving. There was an opportunity at one to write the names of our dead ones. Others were anti-Iraq war, and anti-police brutality. And the special one for me was honouring of all the children who had been miscarried or stillborn. It had been a long time since I'd thought of my four unknown little ones.

We sat on the benches and discovered in five minutes that we were almost beside two of our other sisters from Crete – none of us knowing the others would be there. Reunion and rejoicing! Then came fascinating theatre/ritual in dance and music, followed by a long guided visualisation about the meeting with and letting go of our dead ones. The climax was the Spiral Dance itself. Their years of practice showed as something like 1200 people were somehow connected into a single spiral line with the leaders in the centre.

An amazing feat! Starhawk led the line outwards, and in the half-hour that followed, we must have had close encounters with every other person who was spiralling. It was an enormous experience to be joined physically, emotionally and spiritually with so many others wanting good for the world and each other.

And we chanted:

> Let it begin with each step we take.
> Let it begin with each change we make.
> Let it begin with each chain we break.
> Let it begin each time we awake!

And then the community's new babies were presented as we sang 'For each child that's born, a morning star rises and sings to the universe who we are…'[27]

And so eventually to herchurch and the conference! Architecturally it is an unremarkable suburban parish church, but a sign across the front proclaiming 'God loves all Her children' brought me up short. Why should it feel so 'naughty' and 'risky'? And at the same time so totally right! This is the only official parish I know of where the liturgical language consistently uses feminine images for the Divine. The words God and Goddess are used inter-changeably, women's writings are used for Sunday readings, and scripture-based hymns are sung to Mother Eagle and Divine Midwife. I could worship in my own language! In my own culture! It felt quite amazing. No blocks, nothing to resist. No translations or rewordings needed. Just freedom, authenticity and flow! And I was deeply moved to be asked the first Sunday I was there to read Edwina Gateley's poem *God ran away when they shut her up in a box called church*, and even more so for the conference Eucharist to be asked to read my own poem *Cairn*[28]. I loved Carter Heyward's wonderful Eucharistic prayer about women and making bread and power and blessing, and the loaf round like a pregnant belly… A celebration of freedom and womanhood!

Someone who made a deep impression on me was the assistant pastor Megan, a 27 year-old lesbian, who was ordained as pastor to the homeless of San Francisco, and spends five days of Lent each year living on the streets with her parishioners, and as they do relying on begging for basic sustenance. A dynamic, funny and challenging speaker, who draws on her own experiences of being marginalised to minister to others. The seventy or so attenders at the conference were women and men clergy, academics (Professors of Religious Studies and Women's Spirituality at various universities), theologians and thealogians, artists, musicians, dancers, and ordinary women and men who think language about God is vitally important. Rev Jann Aldredge-Clanton, a Southern Baptist minister and thealogian, was the main speaker, and it was her hymns we sang from her *Liberating Hymns for Inclusive Christians*.

What a rich jewel-box of memories! What profound spiritual food! What freedom in worshipping as one must! The Crete experience continues.

2007

Take this Bread[29]

Her conversion experience was not just unexpected – it was unwanted, even embarrassing! A 49 year-old woman followed an impulse to enter a San Francisco church one Sunday morning in 1999. All the people there were

offered communion so she received as well. Then, in her own words 'Jesus happened to me!' Sara Miles was a committed atheist, a lesbian mother, a journalist, a cook, with a track record of peace work and social activism. She had a significant distaste for organised religion which was shared by her family and friends. Yet she found herself shaken and in tears as she ate this Food that was the Body of Christ. Then there were months of confusion and soul-searching through the labyrinths of bread-food-hunger-Jesus-Mystery-incarnation-community-giving-and-receiving. She was baptised at the church of St Gregory of Nyssa in 2000.

St Gregory's Episcopalian church seems like a building in which such things can happen! The entrance doors lead into a rotunda in the centre of which stands the round altar table. The walls rise to where 99 larger-than-life dancing saints are all following in step with Jesus, Lord of the Dance. A most varied bunch with golden halos: women, men, children and a few animals, multi-national, multi-faith, from the beginning to now: a naked Eve holds hands with Desmond Tutu, the only depicted one still living. Another panel celebrates Sojourner Truth, Bartholome de la Casa, Miriam, Origen, Malcolm X, Elizabeth I, Iqbal Masih and Teresa of Avila! Google the unfamiliar names and prepare to be inspired! High overhead round the cupola are inscribed Gregory's words: 'The one thing truly worthwhile is becoming God's friend'.

To the right is a more usual church space – a few rows of seats facing each other, the lectern stands where the spaces join, and the presider's chair is below a breath-taking mural in the same icon style. At the bottom of the frame Gregory of Nyssa sits preaching. At the top, Mother Sophia presides over the central image of the marriage between Jesus and the Soul. Gregory (331-396) who wrote from his own experience of married love explained that in mystical union with Christ, the 'mother-in-law' of each of our souls is God. He was one of the last married bishops. He too dances on the wall, arm-in-arm with his wife Theosebia.

As Sara explored her new life as a Christian with all its complexities, the simplicity of a call became clear: she and others at St Gregory's were to feed people. Feed the people who were hungry. Feeding people and being fed by others, however poor, had been a core part of her life in many parts of the world, notably war-torn Central America. She pondered the experiences of being fed by and from her mother's body, and of feeding her daughter likewise from her own. And the 'intolerable' instruction from Jesus to eat his body became her central connection to all the other experiences. She was hooked on Eucharist and its consequences! So with support from the congregation she began a food pantry at the church to feed the hungry in their area. The pantry opened its doors the same week as her baptism.

It was a huge learning curve to get this operation running effectively. She had seen publicity from the San Francisco Foodbank, and that set the whole project in motion. This was set up as a redistribution agency 20 years ago for the enormous amounts of food being wasted and destroyed in the US. Through it farmers can donate surplus crops and get tax-breaks. It also gathers seasonal surpluses and donations of food into its massive warehouse, then distributes it to 600 agencies across the area, including St Gregory's. So St Gregory's is part of a much bigger picture.

Sara's first communion was nine years ago. Now 600 hungry people a week come to the central area of the church to receive their food. The altar is covered by a plastic tablecloth. The food comes. The volunteers come. The homeless, the marginalised, the poor ones, the isolated of the area come. They are fed. Many of the volunteers were themselves initially recipients who have found self-respect, community and purpose at St Gregory's. One beamed as she told how energised she feels by doing her volunteer duty. This is all achieved for a financial outlay of $1 per person. And major funding support from donors has enabled St Gregory's to seed another 17 pantries round the area, with passed-on donations and training of volunteers. The work grows!

And on the altar base below the plastic tablecloth in gold lettering: 'Did not the Lord share the table of publicans and harlots? So then… do not distinguish between worthy and unworthy. All must be equal in your eyes to love and serve.' On Sundays, that's how it is. The Liturgy of the Word is held in the chancel, then everyone processes to surround the altar. It is proclaimed: 'Jesus welcomes everyone to his table so we offer his Body and Blood to everyone without exception'. Then they do. The final hymn is danced around the altar in step with Jesus and the saints high around their walls. There is continuity here between liturgy and service.

Sara's integration into and commitment to the Christian community has deepened. Jesus is real, and no longer embarrassing. Friends and family have adjusted to her new life. There are new friends and a new family as well. She has inspired many with her book *Take this Bread*. It inspired me too. Visiting St Gregory's recently, seeing the Food Pantry in operation, and meeting the passionate, earthed woman who responded to the invitation to receive Eucharist and live its consequences was a soul-deep interlude of the Christ who welcomes all.

2008

Desert Stories

They call it the Red Centre. And red indeed it is! Red earth, red monoliths when they infrequently appear, red corrugated roads for as far as the eye can see. We were going as students to a very different learning space, as guests of a Pitjantjatjara clan of Aboriginal Australians. They call themselves Anangu. And they speak Pitjantjatjara which is one of the 250 or so surviving linguistically separate languages of indigenous people in Australia.

Yet another friend enticed me on this astonishing trip, after we'd been together to a shamanic workshop earlier in the year.

Endless spaces with a sparse covering of scrub, now and then a line of gums in a dry river bed, more frequent groves of young desert oaks, standing like fringed pencils a couple of metres high. The occasional dingo. Bands of wild camels, the equivalent of super-sized rabbits, but not enough resources or people to tackle the problem. Their forebears were once the only transport into this remote area but when road, rail and air travel arrived they were simply turned loose. And thrived.

We travelled by a four-wheel drive mini-bus from Alice Springs, with a stop for a brief acquaintance with Uluru/Ayers Rock and a dramatic unexpected sunset on a grey day. Then headed over the border into South Australia and few hundred kilometres west into the Homeland of our hosts.

We were briefed along the way with an introduction to aboriginal thought and understanding of the earth. The exploits of the ancestors produced the landscape. Those stories as they are retold, sung and celebrated are keeping the landscape in existence. Creation has to be continually revitalised by the spiritual attention of the people. The ancestors are not of the distant past, but of the now in a timeless way. This has echoes of the Jewish understanding of their stories: Exodus and Passover are a continuous present into which the community re-immerses itself each year.

And so we met Lee Bradey and his wife Leah, who took us digging for maku (witchetty grubs). Which we ate when they'd been cooked on the fire. Tasted all right, almost like sweet corn. It's the idea that's still a bit of a problem! They live in the roots of a particular shrub, and have to be extricated with considerable effort for not a lot of food. But that was the story of the traditional women's lives. They were the gatherers and the men were the hunters. Their kitchen gear consisted of a digging stick, a wooden bowl and a grinding-stone. Witchetty grubs, high in protein, were what the babies were weaned onto. We heard the stories and engaged with the inma (ceremonies) of the Wati Ngintaka (Perentie Lizard Man) who created, and creates still, the landscape of the area. We were on a pilgrimage along their Songline, with stops at the places where the various incidents are still embedded and embodied in the rocks, caves and waterholes.

We were sleeping in canvas swags under the stars and, miles from any towns, they were scintillatingly awesome. And the very chilly desert dawns were spectacular. As was the morning display of pink underwings as the flock of galahs took off from the gums. It had been a relief to hear that because it was winter all the snakes and scorpions were already hibernating! The flies weren't. At the second campsite we were introduced to Peter Nyaningu and his wife Mildred. He had already been described to us as a 'first contact' person, the term for those who can remember their first meeting with a white person. It seems he is about 75, and was probably 7 or 8 when his father guided whitefella photographer ethnologist Charles Mountford into the area of the Mann Range around 1940. There's a great photo of Peter's dad in his traditional splendour. And we learned that if you don't wear clothes, you don't have pockets, so the traditional hunters carried their precious kangaroo sinews and other small possessions in their hair, in a type of chignon called pukuti.

Peter and Mildred sat with us round the camp fire. It was something of a surprise to hear him begin speaking by preaching the Christian Gospel. He spoke of Jesus and of Moses. And told us how he'd run away from the mission school in Ernabella as a child, but returned as an adult, had studied theology and had been ordained as a Presbyterian minister in 1984.

He pulled out of his case two red books. One was called *Tjukurpa Palya*, and featured a cross. We already knew 'palya' as a most useful word: 'hello', 'thank you', 'good', 'ok', 'right?'. And that 'Tjukurpa' is a most profound word which encompasses their creation story, the sacred foundation of spiritual law, lore and practice, and much more. The combination was new to us. The companion book's title was the familiar *Good News*. Peter's two bibles had helped him learn English as he worked from the Pitjantjatjara edition to the English one and back again.

There were several full page illustrations in colour. The depiction of the first chapter of Genesis has a black Adam and Eve, koalas in a gum tree, a dingo, emu, kangaroo, and platypus. And, somewhat strangely, in this delightful piece of inculturation, a zebra and an antelope! Moses was mentioned again and again, and it was not hard to understand the appeal to Anangu of stories of a leader who led his people out of oppression and into freedom in the desert. The table of contents listed amongst the others Matthew-ku, Markaku, Luke-aku, John-ku, Paulalu. I was intrigued to know whether or how he fitted together their traditional Anangu stories with his Christian understanding, so asked 'Peter, do you have two stories, then?' His response was to clasp his hands with fingers interlaced and say 'They are like this!' and 'God created the ancestors'.

Another story was about the local section of the Seven Sisters Songline, which runs the length of the whole country. We saw the cave where, guided by the wise eldest sister, they had hidden from Wati Neru, a strangely endowed man who 'only wanted to talk to them'. They did not trust him, and eventually escaped to be stars in the sky where he pursues them still. They are our Matariki. We sat in stunned silence in this cave, and later in another, in the presence of paintings depicting this story and others, dating back 20,000 or more years. Very few artefacts anywhere in the world can claim this age.

For probably 60,000 years the aboriginal people have lived on this sub-continent, in the ultimate of sustainable life-styles. They have been reliant totally on the slim pickings from the harsh land, with an appreciation of this dependence, and knowing the responsibility to live in tune with the creative Spirit of the earth. So much that western consumer society can learn from these people! And the knowledge is at risk of disappearing.

Before we parted, Peter drew their Songlines in the sand with his stick, then the state boundaries between Northern Territory, South Australia and West Australia. 'They cut across the Songlines.' Peter said with real anguish, 'The whitefellas made new lines and they broke our Songlines. They stole our land.' It is one thing to know about the history of our neighbour's indigenous people. Quite another to experience the pain now of a real person with a name, and his family! And the generosity of their teaching and sharing. It was good to hear that an increasing number of Australian secondary schools, notably Catholic girls' colleges, are making the pilgrimage to meet these Anangu and hear how it was before, how respect for the ancient way of life has something to offer to us white ones.

Later Lee and Leah shared their Christian faith too. Their travelling music in their van was a CD of the young people of the tribe singing gospel songs in Pitjantjatara. And Leah's Tjukurpa Palya, much thumbed, was on the dash-board.

In his book *The Songlines*[30], Bruce Chatwin writes 'By spending his whole life walking and singing his Ancestor's Songline, a man eventually became the track, the Ancestor and the song.' So close to the words of Jesus: 'I am the Way, the Truth and the Life'.

The Government's apology to Australia's original people was given in 2008 for the centuries of theft, oppression, and disregard. A more recent enquiry found that things have got worse for them, not better. The Anangu of the Pitjantjatjara lands are reaching out to the whitefellas to offer bridges to understanding that can help narrow the gap between white and black in Australia. When what they have to offer in their stories, customs and spiritual care for the earth is received with respect and thankfulness, healing can follow.

2009

Kōhanga

The tree
Deeply rooted in the whenua
Has died
Stark white against the mountain green

The tamariki
Whose whenua nourish that earth
Are alive
They spark and sing

With the tūī
They chant the lovely names
Of River marae
Koriniti, Ranana, Hiruharama, Pipiriki

Fledglings
In their nest learn tikanga
Karakia, waiata
From aunties, koro, and the mums

Their roots
Go deep and as the old tree fails
New saplings spring
Of kahikatea the fire tree

2007

Then a pilgrimage nearer home: a group of spiritual directors walked to Hiruharama, our Jerusalem, on the Whanganui River. A visit to a Māori language marae pre-school was impressive.

Wairua

Wairua-drawn to walk together
Wairua-borne up tranquil river
Wairua-led along the long long road
Wairua-cooled with welcome gentle breeze
Wairua-fed with food prepared with love
Wairua-washed in deep cool pools
Wairua-touched with kindness shared around
Wairua-taught with learnings on the way
Wairua-housed for sleeping starry nights
Wairua-fired by Hemi and Suzanne[31]
Wairua-called to write and love yet more
Wairua-joined in richly woven kete
Wairua-held in memories deeply shared
Wairua-blown renewed to daily dance
Wairua-loved now and forever
Amene

2007

Another Whanganui reflection. Wairua, the Spirit, was in it all.

Pacific Stories

Pacific Stories

This begins at home in Aotearoa, loving the land we belong to, celebrating the city where I've lived for over half a century. Its contours are almost as familiar as my own. Then there's a local historical detective story that took several years to unfold from the day I first wondered 'Why?'

Only as an outsider can I know something of the sense of the pain Māori feel over the loss of land and identity. I discovered similar stories in San Francisco and New Caledonia, and the different struggles in Fiji. First Peoples sharing their stories of oppression, their calls for justice, and human and land rights. The Gospel Jesus through all this saying 'I come that they may have life and life to the full', proclaiming liberty to captives, new sight to the blind – the colonisers could be included here. My eyes have been further opened. Those were my people who did the colonising. These are stories of our neighbours, with whom we share an island, an ocean, a planet. Their wellbeing is crucial to that of the whole global community. They have much to teach us when we are ready to hear.

Papatūānuku

Papatūānuku stirs
My land shakes and rattles
as she reminds us
we are small and temporary
and the cataclysm
can come at any time

Papatūānuku writhes
Inner world crumbles
under the shock
All I knew is gone
Can new things grow?
Small green shoots appear

Papatūānuku trembles
Her wrinkles deepen
as communities talk past each other
over the fringe of her garment
She grieves this cataclysm
after which all is different

Papatūānuku breathes
Peace to all who care
And work for her protection
Rewarding love with love
Ground of our being
Our Mother

2007

We must reverence
our earth,
Papatūānuku,
acknowledge her
pain and wisdom.

Wellington Essay

A feature article for the *Dominion Post* series. 'Home' is sacred, roots are sacred.

Next year I'll be celebrating fifty years as a Wellingtonian. We disembarked here from *TSS Captain Cook* in June 1952, in the worst southerly in twenty-five years. Those forbidding mountains we passed on the way into the harbour were nothing like the pictures of rolling green fields and happy sheep we thought we were coming to! Then straight across in gale and rain onto the Limited for an uneasy train ride north. No-one had told my parents about the desirability of hiring pillows! And a bus to our destination in Tauranga, where we began to learn to be Kiwis.

In 1958 my father got a position in the long-gone General Post Office in Featherston St. He came home from the interview and reported to us that in Wellington sometimes the next-door neighbour's roof was at your basement level. This seemed quite far-fetched to a teenager born to a Lancashire semi-detached home, and living in a flat street in Tauranga, but was proven to be, if anything, an understatement! I was looking forward to all the new experiences of the capital city, but had a lurking fear that it would be a concrete jungle with nary a blade of grass in sight. I still had another year of secondary school to do, and the family's move was in part so I wouldn't have to leave home to attend university.

School provided a number of culture shocks: I was enrolled at St Mary's College for 1959. While I was used to the panama hats and uniforms of Tauranga College, wearing gloves was something else! White in summer, black in winter. Not to be removed while in transit, even on the train I rode to and from Trentham. And whereas bikes were the main form of transport to school in Tauranga, not one solitary person rode to school at St Mary's. In fact no-one anywhere in Wellington in those days rode bikes. Tram tracks, hills and bikes were not a good mix! And wearing slippers in school seemed quite extraordinary. The nuns still wore habits then, only went out in twos, and did not perform in public. I was fascinated by the school concert where a sentry-box affair stood centre stage, in which choir mistress Sister Mary Winifred was ensconced before we started singing, and into it her flowers were delivered at the end!

To my delight Wellington was anything but a concrete jungle – parks, bushy places like Otari, gardens and trees in the centre city, always beautifully tended. I grew to love the hills – for the views from the various vantage points, and for the exercise involved in even short walks. I'm sure Wellingtonians as a breed are fitter than the denizens of Christchurch!

But back to the late 50s and early 60s. There were all sorts of interesting people around. Pat Lawler, dapper and gracious in dark suit and hat. A bedraggled postman who was said to be an alcoholic and a poet. Classmates whose mothers had known each other at school a generation back, whose grandmothers had known Eileen Duggan or Katherine Mansefield. All quite amazing to an immigrant, this network of connections, present, and going back through the previous fifty or even a hundred years.

My university years in the early 60s produced good memories, and memorable folk. Dr Erich Geiringer swishing around in his black cloak, our Classics professor from Aberdeen, who rolled Latin poetry lovingly from his tongue; the solitary woman with academic standing then, Associate Professor Joan Stevens of the English Department. There were only four women students in first year law in 1960! Easterfield was the newest block, and the library and cafeteria were in the Hunter Building. How times have changed!

They've changed in so many other respects, particularly for women. We were expected to resign from the Public Service when our pregnancies became evident. Going to work in maternity clothes was simply not acceptable! No daycare either. But fewer choices did keep things simple – far less juggling than today's women have to do.

I loved walking from Highbury to the top of the Cable Car with my baby in his pram. The beautiful old turreted Skyline building was still there then, and a simple high shed at the terminal. It was easy to ride down the hill with baby still in the pram after the driver had helped me hoist it aboard. This was an easier option than having to remove baby and covers, and hook the pram on the back end of the bus. Buggies hadn't been invented!

Wellington's new motorway in the 70s produced an interesting family project for us. The gravestones from Bolton St Cemetery were stacked like dominoes in the Karori Cemetery while construction was proceeding. Many were subsequently relocated back into the landscaping, but while they were stored, an army of volunteers recruited by the Historic Places Trust recorded all the inscriptions. The Victorian colonial tributes gave far more background and social history than today's monuments do. We became adept with scrubbing brushes and talcum powder to access overgrown or worn lettering.

This led to a later recording of extant stones in Mount Street Cemetery near Victoria University. One in particular intrigued me: a young man who had been drowned in the 'Witangi River in the Provinse of Otago' in 1857. So why was he buried in Wellington? He was described as son of Sir John Lawson of Brough Hall, Yorkshire. I did some detective work, contacted the family who still lived in their ancestral abode, and eventually had the privilege of putting lots of jigsaw pieces together and writing Henry's story. (See p100)

In the 80s I was bringing up a family and came to appreciate Wellington as a community of communities. It wasn't a big impersonal city – each suburb had its village feel. People knew each other. In Northland there were street parties when residents left and there were new neighbours to meet. The local grocer was appreciated when he let parents know about his concerns about their kids. Parents let each other know too! Plunket, Play Centre and Kindergarten committees, cubs, scouts and brownies, babysitting clubs provided social networks for parents and their children.

In the 90s I moved further north again, and came to know the community feel of Johnsonville. Now from my lookout in Broadmeadows, I again love watching the comings and goings in the harbour, the colours and changes of the water and mountains. I am as besotted with Wellington as I've ever been and cannot imagine living anywhere else! It is a joy to have (or find!) visitors who are willing to be shown the vibrant centre city, be taken round the Marine Drive, then up to the wind turbine, or to the summit of Kaukau! Then they too fall in love with Wellington. Which is as it should be!

2008

Henry Lawson's Story

In Mount Street Cemetery, near Victoria University in Wellington lie many of the early sons and daughters of the Catholic Church of New Zealand. There are the well-known and much loved, such as Father JJP O'Reily who lies on the crest of the hill, and Father Jean Baptiste Petitjean. Fr O'Reily was the first resident priest of Wellington, beloved for his charity and respected for his learning. Fr Petitjean was one of the first group of French Marists – a real missionary who in his 37 years of service to the Lord in New Zealand walked most of its length, from Whangaroa in the north to Foveaux Strait in the south. And there are the obscure and unremembered. In the lower section of the cemetery is a sandstone monument, with the grave surrounded by an iron paling fence.

> Our history is important too. A happy interlude working on a family project became a fascinating detective story. It became my first published article, in the long-gone *NZ Tablet*.

It is just possible to make out the worn lettering on the sandstone – to discover that a young man of noble birth nobly met with death:

> Pray for the soul of Henry Lawson, second son of Sir William Lawson of Brough Hall in the County of York. He was drowned in the swollen waters of the River Witangi in the Provinse of Otago on the third day of January 1857 in the 24th year of his age in the attempt to save the life of his drowning shepherd. Greater love than this no man hath, that a man lay down his life for his friends. John CXV, v 15.

There is always something special about a person who gives their life for another. Who was this Henry Lawson, and why was he buried in Wellington when he had died some 600km to the south? These questions have taken several years to be answered, and the picture has emerged of a man who could well be claimed to be a saint and martyr of our early days. The starting point of the search was Burke's Peerage and Baronetage where his family was listed as still living in the ancestral home. A letter to the current baronet brought an exciting reply from Ben Worthington, his son-in-law. The bereft mother, Lady Clarinda Lawson, on receiving the news of her son's death had compiled an album in his memory. Mr Worthington was prepared to send this to me with a friend who was staying with him, coincidentally from Wellington, and about to return. The precious black book arrived and the picture started to build. Henry was an aristocratic-looking young man with a gentle loving nature – page one has, as well as a portrait, some tiny pressed flowers he picked for his mother in Pecknell Wood not long before his departure for New Zealand.

In keeping with the tradition of his very Catholic family, dating back to 1500, Henry had been educated by the Jesuit Fathers in Nice, France. Of his three brothers one became a priest, and all his three sisters were nuns.

Henry landed in the new South Island town of Lyttelton on the *Grasmere* on 4th May 1855. The next we hear of him is in December 1856 when he bought the licence for Run 17 in North Otago, bordered by the Waitaki (the Witangi of the tombstone), the Otekaike and the Maerewhenua Rivers. He took up his sheep station, hired a couple of brothers named McLean as shepherds, and invited a friend up to stay. No doubt they would have climbed to the highest point of the rolling acres to admire the panoramic view, with the Waitaki River stretching away out to the Pacific coast. Good land and a good future!

Three weeks later, in high summer, in that area where water can be so scarce, Henry was drowned. They were dipping sheep in the Washpool in the Otakiroa Creek near the Takiroa Cliffs. These were of interest to the traveller then as now – Māori rock drawings dating back to about 1400 AD decorate the base of the cliffs, and recorded by Mantell, one of the early surveyors in his travel notes of 1848. No doubt Henry with his own richly recorded family history going back to the same era would have been intrigued by this corner of his property.

That day a sheep lost its footing. One of the McLean brothers – whose name was also Henry, and he too was 23 – dived at it and got out of his depth. He could not swim, nor could his brother who called out to Henry Lawson who must have been nearby. Henry tossed off his hat, and confident of his own strong swimming plunged in, coat, boots and all. Henry McLean in panic seized his would-be rescuer, and as related in a letter to Wellington 'they both sank to rise no more in life'. The two bodies were recovered some hours later and as the *Lyttleton Times* reported 'although Dr Rayner who was a guest of the unfortunate gentleman was promptly in attendance, life was of course extinct'.

Mr Daniel Lawlor of neighbouring Otakika Station was a Catholic, and he wrote to Fr O'Reily in Wellington to tell him the sad news and ask for the prayers of the community there. He mentions that he had also written 'to my sisters in Nelson to beg the prayers of the Roman Catholic Congregation there for him – I am sure Mr Garin will have him prayed for in chapel'. This letter, the first item in Lady Clarinda's album, was written the day before Mr Lawlor and a Catholic workman buried Henry Lawson and Henry McLean on top of a cone-shaped hill near the Maerewhenua River, as there was no Catholic priest or church in the province.

Also in this letter, we get a glimpse of Henry as a person of deep spiritual convictions:

> Poor Mr Lawson was a most earnest Catholic – and most attentive to his religious duties so far as the nature of such essentials permitted being practised in this remote district... he had been most attentive to his morning and evening devotions and his respect of Friday and fast day restrictions – on his person was (sic) found an Agnus Dei, a miraculous medal, a Rosary beads and a crucifix.

Fr O'Reily obviously forwarded this letter to the family, no doubt accompanied by some consoling message of his own. Fathers O'Reily and Petitjean must have found joy in Henry's visits to Wellington. Fr Petitjean wrote to the family that on his last visit, when Henry had been delayed by a storm, he said,

> 'I know not when I can receive the Holy Sacrament again, I must have the happiness to communicate this time once more' – and so he did, thus taking a double provision for a long journey, the journey to Eternity.

At this time it was most unusual for a layman to receive Communion on a daily basis. On this visit he had visited Sir Charles Clifford whose family had close connections with his. They too were staunchly Catholic Yorkshire landed gentry. It seems likely that during Charles' visit to England, 1848-50, he could have fired the teenage Henry's imagination with his talk of the possibilities of sheep-farming in the new colony, and even encouraged him to emigrate. With his cousins William Vavasour and Frederick Weld, Clifford had been in at the very beginning of sheep farming in this country. He was elected the first Speaker of the House of Representatives in 1854.

His position in the colony no doubt meant that when Henry visited Wellington he would have been mixing with the notables of the town. On May 15th 1857, shortly after news of the accident reached England, Fr Walter Clifford, a Jesuit, cousin of Charles, and the Lawsons' family chaplain, preached at the memorial service for Henry in their chapel of St Paulinus.

When news of the accident was received, a letter was promptly dispatched to the colony with instructions that could only come from a family of strong convictions and adequate funds: Henry Lawson was to be disinterred from the hasty grave on the hill in Otago, and his body brought to Wellington to be buried on consecrated ground with the full rites of the Church. Here was the key to the mystery of Henry's Wellington grave. Although the reburial merited only a few lines in the *N.Z. Spectator* of July 29th 1857, it must have caused quite a stir in the town:

> On Monday afternoon the remains of the late Henry Lawson Esq (which were brought from Waitangi in the *Lady Grey* last week) were interred in the Catholic Cemetery, Wellington. The funeral left the residence of C. Clifford, Esq. and was very numerously attended, C. Clifford, Esq., with his son and N. Levin Esq attending as chief mourners.

That same day Mary Ann, Clifford's wife, conveyed some consoling and surprising details to Henry's parents:

> I think it will comfort you to know that every office of the Church has been performed over your dear son's remains… I have just returned from the Church where most of the Catholics and a large number of Protestants attended.

> The noble act with which he ended his life made everyone anxious to shew every mark of respect – even to the lowering of the flag at the Government house, a thing which I never before saw done.

The body had been buried in a wooden coffin on 5th Janry – it was removed to Wellington after being in the ground 6 months – the coffin had in places decayed – the length of time it took to remove it from its first place of burial to Wellington was a voyage of one week. When the coffin was opened at Wellington the body was found quite perfect, free from the slightest bad smell, and he looked as though he was only sleeping – but a little paler than in life.

While this account of bodily preservation is surprising particularly in view of the death by drowning, it is not unprecedented. The bodies of many saints have remained incorrupt. However Mrs Clifford's letter conflicts with the local tradition which says the men were buried on the hill without coffins. There is no way to verify either aspect of her story.

Sir William and Lady Clarinda had not heard the last from their son's friends in New Zealand. On February 18th 1858 Fr Petitjean wrote to them to tell them of his love for Henry and his visit to the area where he had lived and died. Fr Petitjean accumulated an impressive record of journeying around the South Island in the days when it was a choice between foot and horseback, and the rivers were unbridged. Some time between June and November 1857 he travelled between Christchurch and Dunedin and must have diverted to make the visit recorded in his letter:

I went to the Station lately occupied by your lamented son… I knew and loved him tenderly. I went to every spot which was of some melancholy interest, his house, his resting place, but particularly to the little stream where out of sheer heroic charity he perished. My grief took me to the grave where he had been first deposited and there poured out a fervent prayer for the repose of his noble and virtuous soul.

He records Henry as saying 'There is no fear' just before throwing himself into the water. He continues to extol Henry's unusual virtue and piety, including his daily Rosary. And 'I was able to procure a lock of his hair – I send it to you… offering… the sentiments of my sincere condolence'.

In Yorkshire too there were many concerned to console the Lawsons for Henry's loss. A stained glass window for the Chapel of St Paulinus was suggested and 'not only Catholics, but Protestants and neighbours of all ranks, both rich and poor, showed an anxiety to contribute towards the memorial'. Lady Clarinda busied herself with the memorial album, including newspaper clippings, mementos of his childhood, and carefully copying by hand the letters received from New Zealand and the sermon of Fr Clifford's. An unknown hand penned an eight verse poem typical of the period beginning:

When the helpless one lay 'neath the dark waters sinking
O thine was the heart and the arm that would save;
For regardless of life, and with courage unshrinking,
Thou didst rush to his rescue and share in his grave!

In Wellington another reminder was being prepared for the family, a watercolour painting of the grave with its headstone and iron-paling fence. In the background is a corner of the verandah of Fr O'Reily's house. At the bottom corner are the initials C.D.B. – Charles Decimus Barraud, one of New Zealand's valued early artists. Was the painting of the grave commissioned, or was he too a friend of Henry's, paying his own tribute?

In the years since that painting was done, the scrub around the grave has grown into a canopy of trees, the house has long since disappeared, Victoria University has mushroomed around the cemetery, and the bare hills are now covered by the homes of Kelburn. Henry's story too was almost covered by the moss of time. But its rediscovery points to the conclusion that North Otago numbers a man of unusual sanctity amongst its pioneer sons.

1982

Postscript

After this story had been recorded, a family member of Henry's came to visit me from their Yorkshire estate where Henry grew up. I later visited them there. They had recently discovered that his brother John, the Jesuit, had been sent to convert the Marquesas Islands, had married the king's daughter and produced a whole line of descendants, now belatedly acknowledged in the official family annals.

Alcatraz – the other story

Islands in harbours have a mystique of their own. Matiu/Somes has had a varied career in its long human history. It was described recently (*DomPost* 1 Jan 08,) as 'a curiously Kiwi Alcatraz', referring to its time as an internment camp in World War II. However, the connection goes even deeper: in December 2007, Matiu/Somes was returned to Wellington iwi, along with the other islands of Te Whanganui o Tara/ Wellington Harbour.

After my 2006 pilgrimage to Crete, I visited some of the good women at herchurch in San Francisco. This call for justice by another indigenous people was new to me, and I felt privileged when the story appeared in *Mana*, the Māori magazine.

A recent visit to the original Alcatraz in San Francisco harbour was a time to learn of the poignant story of this other island claimed by its indigenous people. It was named Isla de los Alcatraces (seabirds) in 1797, and is of course well known through books and movies for its years as an impregnable prison for hardened offenders. The tides rip round it as they surge through the narrow entrance to the huge harbour. No successful escape was ever recorded from there, though the boat trip from the city takes all of twelve minutes – so near and yet so far!

It is now one of the premier tourist attractions of San Francisco, so much so that booking ahead for a visit is advisable. Thousands come every day. It has been very well set up, with a route guided by head-phone commentary, a history of the prison years, stories of the incorrigibles who were incarcerated there, and their various escape attempts. Bizarrely, a former prisoner was a guest of honour the day we went – signing copies of his life story. How things can change!

The first indication to me of the other Alcatraz story was as we pulled in to the wharf area, and large graffiti on a board announced INDIANS WELCOME. Despite keeping a look out for the three weeks I was in San Francisco, I had seen barely any presence or signs of its indigenous people. So here was something of interest, with its echoes of Bastion Point (1977-78) and Moutoa Gardens (1995). The story we heard was this: when the prison was closed in 1963, the island lay abandoned for some years. In November 1969, 79 Indian Americans, men, women and children, occupied it and reclaimed it as their own. Over the 19 months that followed hundreds more Indians joined the occupation. They were eventually removed by Federal Agents in June 1971.

Thankfully, the fascinating story of this occupation is acknowledged to visitors to the island. A video shows a cross-section of events with a commentary by its leaders. It seems to have been a major event in self-understanding for them both individually and as a First Nation.

A display entitled *WE HOLD THE ROCK* describes the occupation as a stand against broken treaties, broken promises and broken lives suffered by America's native peoples since the arrival of Europeans in the 15th century.

Many consider this non-violent act to have been the pivotal event in the development of the modern Indian rights movement. Quotes on a display board include such comments as:

> It was the awakening for the return to the Indian culture… and to some of the old traditions, some of the old ceremonies.

> Alcatraz encouraged young people to become themselves, as opposed to hiding their Indianness.

> … how to respect one another as Indian people, realise how much knowledge we have, and give it to our young people.

> Out of that fire came all these different people spreading out across the country to do incredible work… I think it was a spiritual awakening of our people.

There is also art work done during the occupation on display in the cell block. Of the boat-load of tourists we came with, only two of us stopped to go into the room where they are hung. They are very powerful witnesses to both oppression and renewed courage. A dramatic and colourful triptych by Mitchell Robles tells the story of the coming of the white man, the deaths of traditions, buffalo and Indian. Another painting has a tree of life being guarded by two women – or is it protecting them? Perhaps both!

The island is bleak, forbidding and lacking any water supply. Even the plants are hostile: spiky agaves and a shrub with thorns growing on its leaves. Who knows what would have happened had the US Government not chosen to remove the last of the occupiers? However, as happens, the forcible end to the occupation fired spirits and determination as they went back to tribal reservation communities to work for the betterment of their people.

This 'other story' of Alcatraz is worthy of record! Matiu/Somes has been returned to its original owners. For the last decade re-planting with native plants has been underway and a population of tuataras established, under the care of the Department of Conservation.

Perhaps one day the restoration of Alcatraz will follow!

2008

The Story of Matiu/Somes [32]

This island in Te Whanganui a Tara was named by Kupe for his daughter or niece Matiu in the 10th century. The first settlement story is that Tara and family occupied Matiu in the 15th century before settling on Te Motu-kairangi (Miramar Peninsula), and it is for him that the harbour was named. The limited resources on the island made it unsuitable for permanent occupation. Stories from the end of the 18th century say Matiu was only occupied temporarily in times of war. Two fortified villages Te Moana a Kura and Haowhenua were erected on Matiu for these times by Ngati Ira, and the terraces are still visible. Matiu was used by Ngati Mutunga and Te Atiawa iwi after they had relocated around the harbour in the early 1800s.

The editor of *Mana* requested the story of our Whanganui o Tara island to accompany the Alcatraz one.

With the arrival of the New Zealand Company and British settlers in 1839, there ensued a period of chaos for the Wellington area, as 'sales' of land were 'negotiated' by Wakefield with local rangatira and iwi. Matiu was included in the Deed of Sale of the Port Nicholson Block. It was renamed Somes Island after Joseph Somes who was the deputy governor of the New Zealand Company.

A lighthouse was erected in 1866 to protect the increasing number of ships using the harbour, and the first lighthouse keeper William Lyall took up residence. There is still a light, but resident keepers were discontinued in 1910.

Islands in harbours are often used for quarantine stations. Somes was first used this way in 1872 when the immigrant ship *England* arrived with cases of smallpox on board. Graves on the island date from this period. A shameful episode in 1904 was the isolation and desertion on Mokopuna Island, just north of Somes, of Kim Lee, a Chinese man, who was suspected of having leprosy. He lived and died in a small cave there, although probably not of leprosy.

Animal quarantine facilities for animals were also constructed on Somes and in use from 1893. By the early 1970s a highly specialised Maximum Security Quarantine Station was built. This massive operation ensured the safe expansion of New Zealand's agricultural industry.

A major shift in the use of Somes Island was the internment there of enemy aliens in both World Wars (1914-18 and 1939-45). During the earlier war, internees were mostly Germans, and during the later one there were Germans, Italians and Japanese. There was a short time in 1943 when a heavy anti-aircraft artillery battery was operational on the island, and internees were moved to Pahiatua. They were returned in 1944. From 1942 to 1945 a degaussing station was operated by Wrens (Women's Royal Navy Service). This was a system of protecting steel hulled ships from mines laid by German raiders by using a magnetic treatment.

Happier times came for the island in the early 1970s when its conservation potential was recognised. In 1981 the Lower Hutt Forest and Bird Protection Society began a habitat restoration programme and established a nursery to provide native plants for revegetating the island. Rats were eradicated in 1989. The animal quarantine station was closed in 1995, and responsibility for the island passed to the Department of Conservation.

In 1997 Matiu/Somes became the island's official designation, acknowledging first its 1000- year significance to Māori, then to Pakeha. Restoring some of its earlier life has proceeded with the reintroduction of the Wellington Tree and Giant Cook Strait Wetas (1996), Brothers Island Tuatara (1998), Kakariki, (2003), North Island Robins (2006), and a variety of skinks and geckos. Rare birds such as the spotted shag also breed on the cliffs. Recently 200 nesting boxes were installed for little blue penguins. Many dedicated members of the public have helped with the work involved. There is a group called Friends of Matiu and a Matiu/Somes Charitable Trust which issues a newsletter three times a year; *Matiu Really Matters*.

These days the existence of a daily ferry service from Wellington and Days Bay,[33] means that it is more accessible to people just wanting to enjoy what is happening there and the different perspective on the harbour.

The Wellington Tenths Trust lodged a claim to the Waitangi Tribunal in 1987. It was representing four iwi, Te Atiawa, Taranaki, Ngati Tama and Ngati Ruanui, who had settled round Wellington in the 1820s and 1830s. The claim was accepted in 2003.

And in December 2007 this was settled in a historic agreement. The ownership of Matiu/Somes, along with Makaro/Ward and Mokopuna, was restored to Māori. The islands will all retain reserve status, and public access will not be changed. The Government is considering reinstating the name Te Whanganui a Tara to be used jointly with Wellington Harbour.

Ngata Love, chairman of the Wellington Tenths Trust and leader of the claim team, is a descendant of rangatira Wi Tako Ngatata and Te Puni from whom the New Zealand Company acquired land in 1839. He said the settlement of this claim, of which Matiu/Somes is a part, would bring great benefits to the claimants whose land was wrongly taken in the 1830s, and called the deal 'an important step forward for the nation'.

2008

Fiji Diary: The Good News!

When I was preparing for a two week holiday staying with Kiwi friends in Suva, I wanted to see who was doing what, what life was really like in the real Fiji. I was there from the end of May 2007, and returned home just before the crisis around the expulsion of the New Zealand High Commissioner. Thanks to my friends there were many fascinating non-standard tourist experiences. While there is a long way to go before stability and human rights can be taken for granted there, there are many wonderful people and organisations doing great work in Fijian society. God is at work in and through their lives!

I'm blessed with friends who made this great patchwork of experiences possible.

There seemed to be at least three different dimensions in Fiji. In one, tourists were safe and happy in their resorts. In another the lives of many people go on as they always have, albeit with some increased tension. But there is a turbulent third layer where danger and political intrigue are rife, and logic, that concept beloved in western doings, has no great value.

Some happenings:

Tuesday: I went with my friend to the foodbank where she is a volunteer. This is run as one of the three arms of the JP Bayly Foundation. JP Bayly (1882-1963) was a Fijian-born European who made a lot of money on property deals. He lived extremely simply – a small house, a box for a table and smaller ones for chairs. In 1954 he set up a Foundation to help the poor of Fiji. It runs food and welfare, medical, and educational services. The income from Bayly's trust provides hundreds of families from both races with the necessities of life. There is a government social welfare benefit, but at $60F a month it simply cannot feed, clothe and educate.

Despite his antipathy for churches, Bayly worked with Anglican priest, doctor and teacher George Hemming to get his dream underway. The work, like the need, has grown. About 3000 families a year are assessed, and given food and clothing. Cheap and free medical care and medicines are available to about 5000 patients a month. If educational support is given it is a commitment for the full extent of the pupil's school days, and includes fees, uniforms, bags and books. A report of a recent prize-giving had some inspirational and deeply grateful young people acknowledging that they had been given a chance to escape from poverty and make their way in the world. About 500 are being helped in any one year. 'Whatsoever you do to the least of my brethren....'

Thursday: We went to the Blue Ribbon Vigil in the Anglican Cathedral of the Holy Trinity to pray for peace and justice in Fiji. This vigil was first held during the coup crisis of 2000, when wives and families – Christian, Hindu and Muslim – gathered to pray for those being held hostage. The ribbons are the colour of the Fijian flag. It was re-started after last December's coup. The day we went most of the regulars were at a meeting, so there were two young Fijian women and the two of us. They were very appreciative of our presence, and we were happy to add our prayers, to wear our blue ribbons, and share the meditation sheet with its words of wisdom from many traditions.

Friday: We met with one of the other food-bank volunteers who is also working on the committee of the Fiji Cancer Society which is setting up the first hospice in Fiji. They have a mammoth task ahead, converting an old ward of the former Suva TB hospital to an 8 bed hospice. Fundraising is in full swing with a planned 'Fiji's Biggest Morning Tea'. Last year's raised $45,000. It has been satisfying to make some Wellington contacts for them.

Saturday: And yes, I was present on the middle Saturday for the now infamous Junior All Blacks game, where Interim Prime Minister Commodore Bainimarama sat a row behind us in the grandstand. We were part of a row of black t-shirted Kiwis, and watched while our High Commissioner, Michael Green inspected the teams, and took his place in the VIP tent on the side-lines at the request of the Fijian Rugby Union. If there was any 'snub' involved, it was their doing, rather than any New Zealand initiative! His expulsion ten days later instigated the next political crisis and further deterioration of relations with New Zealand.

Sunday: My hosts were attending mass at the Catholic South Pacific Regional Seminary, and I did too. The round open sided chapel was a wonderful blend of traditional and local influences.

The tall pointed tabernacle is modelled on a chief's house, and the sanctuary lamp shines inside a large conch shell. Fifty or so dark skinned, white-cassocked young men sang like angels, with hymns in Fijian, Cook Island Māori, and Pidgin. They are about half of the current student roll. So good to see these men being formed in the way of peace and justice!

Monday: The monthly meeting of the International Women's Association was held this time at the Japanese Ambassador's residence, with origami as its focus. The Japanese women looked stunning in their kimonos, and the Indians in their saris. The beautiful big reception room was hung with strings of colourful peace cranes and decorative balls. We all got to try our hand at the ancient art. IWA has a dual focus: it provides a social network for its 150-odd members from 28 countries who mostly have partners working in Suva; and it does fund raising for charity and is of necessity apolitical. Recent projects have been air-conditioning and a television for the children's oncology ward at Suva Hospital. Others have been funding the painting of a school, providing another with a water tank, school books and cervical smear kits.

Tuesday: Before leaving New Zealand I'd heard of Sharon Baghwan Rolls and her work with femLINKpacific. A visit to their Community Media Centre in downtown Suva was both inspiring and thought-provoking. The CMC operates on a non-profit basis to give:

> women, young women and women with disabilities and other marginalized and under-served groups in urban/semi-urban Suva greater access to new and appropriate information, communication technology as well as community media and information materials as a catalyst for empowerment.

One way they do this is to take a 'suitcase radio' to the villages and encourage the women to tell their stories. They are also training young women in media skills, and the office has staff from both the Indo-Fijian and indigenous communities, working together for a common cause. Sharon herself has been nominated for a Nobel Peace prize for her dynamic work for human rights, in particular those of women and children.

During my stay a letter from her appeared in the *Fiji Sun*. The payments to Fijian men who go to be UN peacekeepers in Iraq are bringing comparatively huge amounts in the local economy – so any suggestion that, given the present circumstances, they should no longer be used by the UN is strongly repudiated. Sharon's letter, while acknowledging this role of the military, suggested that equal attention should be given to UN resolution 1325 entitled *Women, Peace and Security*:

> the important role of women in the prevention and resolution of conflicts and in peace-building, and the importance of their equal participation and full involvement in all efforts for the maintenance and promotion of peace and security.

Their latest newsletter (12 July 07) features an open letter from Sharon to the Interim Prime Minister:

> We also express our great concern that military and police personnel are demonstrating a lack of respect for human dignity and the sanctity of human life; We therefore seek your advice, as to what consideration is being given to the need to prepare for a peaceful reformation, and a more clearly defined role of the Republic of the Fiji Military Forces to include its social obligation for the maintenance of security for Fiji citizens that does not involve human rights violation.

She asks: 'what plans does the interim administration have to revive the work facilitated by the New Zealand Government, by Father Michael Lapsley, which was paving the way for a national truth and resolution process?' And quotes Father Lapsley, from an interview with femLINKpacific on 16 November 2006:

> There is a range of human emotions, both positive and negative we share as a human family, and it's on that basis that I think we can learn from other contexts or from other peoples, not to simply exactly reproduce what's done in another context, but to say, can we learn from their triumphs and their tears.

The peace-making process goes on!

Wednesday: I couldn't leave Fiji without a swim in the sea and being on a little island. Even my brief (28 hours), blissful visit to the Toberua resort had its inspirational side. It is off the coast from Nausori, the airport for Suva. It has a mutually useful relationship with two villages on the nearby coast of the mainland. Staff are drawn from there and trained in hospitality. That at least two of them have been employed for over 25 years is a tribute to all concerned! And guests are invited to go from the island on a formal paying visit to the villages for their rural Fiji experience. Everyone gains!

I came away from Fiji with a sense of the enormous amount of solid good work that is being done for those in need, by all sorts of people, ordinary and not so ordinary, and organisations, both church and secular. They are keeping the community ticking over at grass-roots level as best they can. And there are the prophetic ones who speak of a peace based on justice. There is hope for Fiji, that when the prayers are answered and heavy-handed police and military have eventually been reined in, good sense, freedom and peace may yet prevail.

2007

In Memoriam:
Jean-Marie Tjibaou *(1937-1989)*

Twenty years ago on the 4th of May in New Caledonia, a good man was assassinated. Jean-Marie Tjibaou was a man who spoke the soul of his people. His family had already felt the full weight of French colonial oppression. In 1917 during a crackdown on the indigenous people, his grandmother was shot dead by government troops as she carried her four-year-old son, after their village Tiendanite had been burnt down. The child rolled through ferns and was picked up by an older sister. That was Jean-Marie's father. And two brothers were killed in 1984. Kanak land had been systematically taken since the French claimed the island in 1853, and it was not until 1947 that 'the natives' were given the right to vote. There has been significant unrest over land alienation in the colony with various crises since the 1870s.

A long standing wish to visit New Caledonia was fulfilled on another friend's initiative. My rusty French recovered fairly well. And a man I'd never heard of engaged my attention. Another call for justice.

In a recently published biography (Dec 2008), Eric Waddell describes Tjibaou as:

> arguably the most important post-World War II Oceanic leader. His intellectual abilities, acute understanding of both Melanesian and European civilisations, stature as a statesman, commitment to non-violence and vision for Melanesia's potential contribution to the global community have all contributed to the creation of a remarkable and enduring legacy.

Others have described him as having the stature of a Gandhi or Mandela, and believed a Nobel Peace prize would have been a just reward for the work he did for his people.

Jean-Marie Tjibaou was the leader in the move to indigenous (Kanak) self-awareness and political initiatives. He was born in 1937 in the rebuilt village of Tiendanite in the mountains of northern New Caledonia, and received his first schooling from the Catholic missionaries in the Canala area. At 13 he entered the Marist 'little seminary' at Paita, followed by their seminary on the Isle of Pines where he did his novitiate. He was ordained to the Catholic priesthood in Hienghène in 1965, and was appointed to serve in the cathedral parish in Noumea.

In 1968 he went to France, and studied at the Sociology Institute and Catholic University in Lyons. Then he undertook a PhD thesis in ethnology at the Sorbonne in Paris, researching the Kanak cultural identity. He did not complete the academic qualification, but gained a new depth of understanding of what happens to indigenous people under colonisation. He returned to New Caledonia in 1970 for the death of his father, left the priesthood and asked for laicisation, which was granted in 1972. He married Adi and they had four sons and a daughter.

In 1974-5, very passionate about cultural questions and aware of the political potential, he dreamed up and organised the Melanesia 2000 Festival of 1975, where Kanak identity became visible for the first time to its own, to the white French settlers and to the world. He also worked on the publication of Kanaké which expressed the fruit of his study and thinking about his people. In 1977 he was elected mayor of Hienghène. He was on a list called Maxha 'Taking New Pride'. He also became vice-president of the 8th congress of Union Calédonienne. This was the beginning of the radical push for Kanak independence. An Independence Front was formed in 1979, and he was elected to the Territorial Council. In 1982, he was elected vice-president of the New Caledonian Governing Council.

In November1984, he became head of the new Front de Libération Nationale Kanak et Socialiste (FLNKS), and soon became president of the non-legal Provisional Kanaky Government. He was president of the Northern Region of the country in 1985-86.

On 5 December 1984 while he was overseas, two of his brothers were killed in an ambush by white settlers, along with eight other Kanak. His response was after negotiations to order the dismantling of the barricades and no retaliation, based on his belief in non-violence. New Zealand writer James McNeish recounts the story of his 15 year friendship with Tjibaou and the news of those court proceedings in 1986. The seven settlers who had blocked the road with a tree and killed ten unarmed men with their automatic weapons were initially told there was no case for them to answer. McNeish and others challenged this.[34] The case was consequently reopened in 1987, but unsurprisingly the seven were all then acquitted.

In June 1988 after yet another crisis, Tjibaou participated in negotiations in Paris in order to put an end to the further violence of the 'colonial tragedy' which had already cost a number of Kanak militants their lives. These involved meetings at the highest level, with the French Prime Minister Michel Rocard and the Caledonian leader Jacques Lafleur. After the many years of unrest, the signing of the Matignon Agreement restored peace and promised a referendum on independence in 1998. It gave greater local autonomy and redressed some of the deep differences between the lives of the indigenous people and the French colonists. But because the Kanak people are only 42.5% of the population, achieving independence from France still seemed unlikely. Twenty years on New Caledonia/Kanaky is still a colony.

Fr Peter Kiley SM of Wellington remembers meeting Tjibaou briefly in Bourail in 1988 when he was accompanying NZ college students on a school trip. He was deeply impressed by Jean- Marie's charisma. 'He had a remarkable presence, quiet, with a hidden strength. And in the Melanesian way, seemed in accord with nature and himself'. He attended the same Christmas Midnight Mass as Tjibaou. 'The security was amazing, police and army out in force, and bodyguards with him even as he went to Communion.'[35]

Those are the external events of his life. His heart and soul are contained in his writings:[36]

> Kanak means 'man'; it is a Polynesian word. In the myth of Téin Kanaké, Kanaké is the first-born son of the ancestors, he is Man coming into the world.
> The Kanak must speak, his talk must say who we are, and the way the country is organised must be built on the gut words which spring from our soil and the traditional institutions.

> Our land is not for sale, our stolen land,
> Sold land, sold over and over again,
> Is still not for sale, it is our people's unity,
> It is the universe we share with our gods,
> It is the spatial element in our alliance with other related clans,
> It is part of our very existence,
> The vitality we inherit from our ancestors
> Comes to us from the depths of the Earth…

> The Pacific, with its ocean and islands is the gift of the gods to the people of the Pacific, old and new. The ocean, the islands, the air the light the fish, the birds, the plants and Man are the life which is our supreme heritage… We are all responsible in our own way for its fulfilment.

> Kanaké who goes to the Catholic Mass or Protestant services to worship the God of Jesus Christ, has not completely given up his ancestral beliefs. Deep inside himself, he seems to have kept a safe passage to the ancestors.

> The women of New Caledonia, like all the mothers of the world, give birth and keep on giving it at every hour of the day. Maybe that is why, bound to want happiness, they have felt how keenly the problems of the people of their race reach into the very depths of their being.

> I am transient, but I must do my utmost so that the country I will bequeath unto my sons be the most beautiful, one where there is richness, richness of thought, of wisdom, of flowers, of food.

Jean-Marie Tjibaou was assassinated on 4 May 1989, tragically by a Kanak member of a splinter political group who mistakenly thought he had 'sold out' in his negotiations with the French and colonial administrations. His deputy Yeiwéné Yeiwéné was also killed. His friend James McNeish attended the state funeral, and describes how twenty thousand people walked behind the caskets to the cathedral. The white Catholic Archbishop of Noumea knelt and blessed the casket covered with its Kanak flag. Prime Minister Rocard came from France, and wept as he paid tribute before the television cameras. The burial took place at his home village of Tiendanite the following day, near the graves of his father and the ten ambushed ones.

In the bushy outskirts of Noumea, on Rue des Accords du Matignon, stands a most extraordinary building, named for this extraordinary man. The Tjibaou Cultural Centre, built on the site of the 1975 cultural event, celebrated its 10th anniversary in 2008. It was designed by Italian Architect Renzo Piano who was also responsible for the Georges Pompidou Centre in Paris and the Kansai International Airport in Japan. The construction was the culmination of a French government initiative to encourage Kanak cultural expression. Piano works to and with his clients' culture, so ten vertically positioned shell-like structures representing Kanak village ceremonial houses are along a gently curving central alley like the central village pathway. They soar in three groups in varying heights up to 28 metres. And the complex has a deliberately unfinished look to represent the on-going development of Kanak culture. It holds art work by Kanak people and others around the Pacific including Aotearoa New Zealand, and has an extensive library and three theatres.

Outside a Kanak Pathway winds through traditional gardens depicting the culture's symbiotic relationship with the natural world. In the grounds are examples of many Pacific-style buildings. On the hillside overlooking the complex is a larger-than-life bronze statue of Jean-Marie Tjibaou. It is decorated with brightly coloured pieces of cloth, tributes from visitors in the Kanak way. This complex is a centre of Kanak awareness and identity, so appropriately named for this truly inspirational man, leader of his people, and a great human being!

2009

Thinking it Through

Thinking it Through

Sophia Holy Creator has through the evolutionary process equipped us with minds as well as hearts. Thealogy is the woman-spelling for theology, denoting the feminine imaging of the Divine, Thea (Goddess) instead of Theos (God).

By whichever spelling, the process is 'faith seeking understanding', the ongoing search for Truth. How does it all work? Are all the old stories still the best way for 21st century people to be introduced to the eternal truths? What is really happening to real people's lives and faith? How are the handed on Christian traditions and teaching actually impacting on those who hear them? In ways that are healing? Or ways that cause harm to those already struggling? How can the essence of Jesus' teaching be reframed to give the least among us what they need to heal and grow?

Many of the people I've worked with over the last twenty years are unlikely to have spoken their truth directly to theologians. The voices of women subjected to rape, domestic violence and other abuse, people with mental illnesses, long-term beneficiaries are easy to miss, to 'not hear' in the more academic considerations of Life, Truth and God. Through my personal and professional life experience I have been sensitised to these voices, and offer reflections amplifying what I have heard into a different arena of conversation. Truth-seekers and teachers of faith stories must hear all the voices! Once heard, they cannot then with integrity be ignored.

And there are the forays into traditions beyond my own, and the delighted, if sometimes astonished, recognition of our common experience and understanding. As I read it, the different faith traditions are at their core different symbol systems, different efforts to make sense of Life, human beings' dealings with each other and their yearning for the Transcendent. Though, yes, there is the uniquely Christian heritage of being centred on a real, alive-now, historical person. And where does his Mother, the Woman of Faith fit in?

Re-Imaging the Cross

The Cross as the central symbol of our faith has had many profound meanings attributed to it over the centuries that have both helped and hindered those to whom it matters. Symbols, however precious, develop new meanings and shed older ones as times and contexts change.

More and more discomfort with traditional presentations of the Christ story! How else to understand it?

A few years ago I was asked by a young man from an evangelical church 'Are you a Christian?' 'It depends what you mean by Christian', I replied cautiously. If he'd said 'Do you lead a Christ-centred life?' he'd have got an immediate 'That's what I aim for!' But no: his response was to ask 'Do you believe that God the Father sent Jesus to die for our sins?' I pondered a few minutes before replying 'No, I don't think I do'.

In evangelical/charismatic circles where once I worshipped, this statement is the touchstone, the shibboleth: if you can say it, you're in; if not, you're out! So what has happened to my understanding of the cross of Jesus? And not just mine – there are many who have wrestled with the traditional theology and its implications, and have needed to develop a new understanding of the world-changing event of Jesus' death.

I've joined the ranks of those who understand that the image of a g/God who required child sacrifice, or blood sacrifice to atone for sins simply does not work in this third millennium. Paul was the first to record in writing that particular interpretation of the crucifixion of Jesus in that particular way, e.g. Romans 5:6-9. John later articulated the more specific understanding in John 3:16. Paul's time in history was much closer to such rituals than is ours. They were still part of the communal memory of Israel, but are alien to the way we understand the Divine today.

The Romans used the brutal punishment of crucifixion as a matter of course. That it happened to Jesus is undeniable; what it *means* has caused soul-searchings for many in recent times. Many have come to reject atonement theology as simply not working any more, especially as the community has come to grips with the suffering inflicted on children by fathers. I was shocked when I first heard the phrase 'Divine child abuse' as a description of 'God sent His Son to die', but over recent years that has become for me an accurate enough description.

There are also many who have observed that the Christian injunction to 'carry your cross' has been inappropriately used as a way to keep people in life-sapping situations: peasants in poverty, women in violent marriages, blacks under apartheid… A belief that passive suffering is redemptive benefits those in power, not those who suffer. A God of the Exodus who cares enough about those sufferings to want people out of oppression seems a lot more lovable, trustworthy and on the side of the poor! Personal powerlessness is so unhealthy for human-beings, and whatever endorses it is, to use another evangelical phrase, 'not of God'.

The Cross is also implicated in the Christian origin of anti-Semitism, as the Jews were blamed for the death of Jesus. And, since the time of Constantine, it is implicated in militarism, colonising and enforced conversions: the 'God is on our side' and 'We are doing this for God' syndromes.

So what else could the crucifixion mean? Before I discovered others had come to the same understanding, I'd figured that when one speaks out for truth, justice and compassion against the vested interests of the powers-that-be, crucifixion is a highly likely outcome. Crucifixion, literal or metaphorical, happened to the prophets, it happened to Jesus, it happens still. We need only remember the stories of Oscar Romero, Martin Luther King and early complainants to churches about sexual abuse by clergy.

The Catholic Church has moved to being much more Resurrection-focussed since Vatican II. The mass is more often now described as Sacred Meal, rather than as Unbloody Sacrifice, which was the standard description in my youth. But we still need a theology of the Cross that works for people of faith now; on both personal and structural levels. What does it mean? How can its message and significance be re-framed and absorbed into the depths of our souls? And adapted to times where violence is 'never ok'?

For me, the crucifixion and resurrection of Jesus are his trailblazing for us for those times in our lives when absolutely everything we've worked towards lies shattered, finished, destroyed. By the power of Divine Love he transcended that experience, and the same Divine Love is there for us too. It brings life after death, spring after winter, light after dark, healing after devastating pain, and birth after labour.

And on the last of these, it was moving to hear of a local gynaecologist who told a patient, 'If you want to see Jesus on the cross, watch a woman in labour!' The parallels don't stop with the pain: we used to be told that the blood and water that came from his side were the symbolic giving birth to the Church, and then there was the feeding…

Besides the various theologies/beliefs about its meaning, the Cross continues to be a fruitful source for prayerful reflection. On the nailings: how do we fasten Jesus down so that he is unable to walk through our lives to touch and heal? On his thirst: a recognition that he thirsts for each one of us personally. The Cross is sign of the God who suffers with us. Some members of the Disability and Spirituality community speak of a strong identification with Jesus crucified, as the Disabled God who deeply understands the constraints and un-freedoms of their conditions, and is 'in it' with them. And the Cross is a sign of his identification with all marginalised people – he did not simply eat and drink with them, he died criminalised and naked, about as marginalised as a human being can get!

Those for whom the traditional understandings of the Cross holds no problems can continue peacefully in their theology. To those for whom questions and doubts have arisen, know that you are not alone! All of us come to the same Cross, even if we understand it through different windows!

2008

'...as we forgive them...' or not: when forgiveness is inappropriate

For the Auckland Catholic Institute of Theology book on sin/wrong-doing, relaying the experience of traumatised and marginalised people.

Forgiveness, like dynamite, is a potent force, and can cause problems if misused. In the Christian community and beyond, forgiveness is considered the desirable if not imperative response by someone who has been injured to the one responsible. This is understood and transmitted as an important component of the Gospel teaching of Jesus, as a primary characteristic of the whole Christian ethos, and is often contrasted with the lack of this teaching in other faith traditions. It is how we try to avoid the cycle of revenge and bitterness that can be observed continuing for generations in some parts of the world. It is often promoted, particularly in a range of churches, as a necessary step on the route to healing from an injury, with the corollary that refusing to forgive is sinful, makes the injured party bitter and causes further harm.

I too believed wholeheartedly in the necessity of forgiveness as the appropriate response to all injury, until a variety of personal and professional experiences provoked me to have another look. The interface between religious belief and mental health and wellbeing is crucially important, and I believe with Jung that all our emotional difficulties implicate our meanings and values.

In this paper I place alongside normal church teaching – 'forgiveness is a necessary step to healing' – some patterns and situations where this religious/cultural story can cause more harm than good. I outline experiences of victims of sin and violence and those who work with them, identify the sources of the belief in forgiveness as a spiritual necessity, report on a counsellor's workshop on forgiveness, then look at alternatives to the traditional understanding. There are situations where forgiveness is not the morally or humanly appropriate response to injury.

Stories

A woman and her partner many years ago forgave the relative who sexually abused their daughter, after he apologised when confronted and promised it would not happen again. He was not reported to the police. He then went on to a long career of abusing many other children. When this became known, she was angry that her 'Christian duty' of forgiveness had facilitated a much bigger story of abuse and damage. Her relationship with her daughter as both a child and adult was severely damaged, as the daughter perceived the parents as 'doing nothing' about the abuse.

Another woman was afraid to return to her evangelical church after a mental breakdown because, based on her own previous experience, she anticipated pressure from the pastor and people to forgive the man who had raped her. She also expected to be told that the ongoing mental health problems she was having were because she 'wouldn't forgive'.

117

And those who work with women subjected to domestic violence have identified the cycle of violence where apologies, promises, and forgiveness requested and given, often at great cost, become the recurring preludes to further episodes of violence.

Christian teaching

It is easy to identify Christian teaching from all denominations as a primary source of the idea that victims of injuries 'have to forgive', that this is always the appropriate response to injury, for example, the trans-denominational Lord's Prayer ('Forgive us our sins as we forgive those who sin against us'), and Gospel quotes such as, 'Whenever you stand praying, forgive, if you have anything against anyone; so that your Father in heaven may also forgive you your trespasses'(Mk 11:25); 'Forgive and you will be forgiven' (Lk 6:37). These words individually and collectively leave us in no doubt that in order to be forgiven oneself, one must extend forgiveness to others. And who of us does not need to be forgiven? Unforgiveness is itself regarded as a sin.

Some quotes I have personally heard from local ministers of a variety of denominations:

> 'Anyone who refuses to forgive has one foot in hell.'

> 'Anyone who says they have forgiven but not forgotten hasn't forgiven.'

> 'Revenge… is about justice, forgiveness is about love.'

> 'Anyone who doesn't forgive has a cancer in their soul.'

To resist this sort of pressure takes considerable personal courage! However there is burden enough in living with the effects of trauma, without having added to that the guilt at being unable to forgive. I remember my relief when I was struggling with a major life event and a (non-Christian) counsellor first told me, 'You don't have to forgive'. This was a shocking new thought. I say this to clients myself now, and have been moved by the visible difference it can make as the burden of obligation is lifted, and the guilt at 'not being able to forgive' is eased and healing facilitated. One said, 'A ton weight has come off my shoulders'.

Points pondered

When does repeated forgiveness become a form of collusion? Some Christians find it very easy to resort to an unreflected-on Gospel quote: 'Jesus said just keep on forgiving'. We live in different days now, with different understandings of the complexities of human behaviour and the effects of trauma.

When the community wants a victim to forgive, if she/he complies does this remove responsibility for further action from the community? When a victim 'refuses to forgive', how does a community respond? To the perpetrator? To the victim?

In traditional Christian teaching, 'forgiveness' follows 'repentance': genuine acknowledgement of wrong done, expression of regret, serious steps to redress the situation, and intention to not repeat the behaviour. These are the sacramental requirements for absolution in the Catholic sacrament of Reconciliation. What if there is no repentance by the perpetrator?

What does the word 'forgiveness' actually mean? Is it an act, a decision, a journey, an attitude, an aim, a change of heart?

Why is it assumed that if a person hasn't forgiven then they are 'bitter and vengeful'? Rarely does 'seeking accountability and justice' get inserted between these polarities. In fact one minister quoted above equated 'justice-seeking' with 'revenge'.

Has anyone actually the right to urge, expect or advise anyone else to forgive?

Counsellors' workshop

These questions were considered by about 20 counsellors in a workshop I facilitated in 2003, when I took my curiosity about how others see forgiveness to an open conversation. We discovered a significant number of us were from a Catholic background.

We came to some basic agreements:

1. Our personal attitudes to, and experiences with injury and forgiveness influence our approach to clients when forgiveness of an injury is an issue of theirs. They may be struggling with how to forgive, unwillingness to forgive, or guilt at being unable to do so, and the implications of doing so or not.

2. Belief systems must be re-examined and renegotiated to ensure they are life-giving.

3. Forgiveness is contra-indicated if:

   - it is too soon
   - anger and other feelings have been suppressed, especially when there is significant trauma
   - it is under duress/pressure, seen as a moral duty
   - it is part of an abuse cycle
   - it is 'to help the perpetrator' in some way (misplaced compassion)
   - there are addictive behaviours involved
   - it is conditional – for example, in the hope of restored love/acceptance
   - it is for the 'greater good' but damaging to the person
   - some institutional responsibility would be short-circuited
   - there is institutional support for the offending to continue

4. Forgiveness is compatible with laying charges/complaints. This is passing over to the community responsibility for dealing with the offender/offence.

5. The lived-out implications of forgiveness can be somewhere along the continuum from 'full re-commitment to the relationship and re-building trust' (the standard interpretation), through 'moving on', 'letting go', 'unclipping a relationship', 're-deploying energy', 'a deep acceptance of the reality of what has occurred', to simply 'not seeking revenge'.

6. Ideas for helping clients heal:
   - Permission to not forgive
   - Encouraging them to give priority to their own feelings and process (e.g. anger, grief). Where these are suppressed any short-term relief prejudices longer term well-being.
   - Alternative Bible quotes to those requiring forgiveness, for example, the Hebrews did not have to forgive the Egyptians – they were told to get away (Exodus); God is more interested in your recovery than in your ability to forgive (Luke 4:18).
   - Referral to a trained spiritual director if a counsellor is uncomfortable with a client's belief system. Consultation between a counsellor and spiritual director with the client's consent can be helpful.
   - Recognition by the counsellor of developmental stages of maturity and faith, for example, Fowler's Stages of Faith[37]

7. The outcome for the person who forgives can be freedom and peace, a sense of a hold being broken, an ability to re-deploy energy, taking back one's power and strength. They alone can determine the timing.

8. The outcome for a person who sees themselves as withholding forgiveness can be the same.

Scripture and forgiveness

The Gospel quotes on forgiveness can be seen in context, and I now understand that when Jesus was insisting on its necessity, he would have been speaking to men imbued with the philosophy of 'an eye for an eye and a tooth for a tooth' – which itself was an advance on the uncontained and disproportionate revenge of previous eras. He was not speaking to battered women and other traumatised victims of sin! His compassion for the powerless marginalised ones would never have laid this burden on those who had been damaged. The pertinent scriptures for their situations are likelier to be his words in Matthew 12 as he quotes Isaiah 42:3 – about not breaking crushed reeds or quenching wavering flames, and in Matthew 23:4 – about not laying burdens on those already struggling.

Power and gender issues

How does the power imbalance between a victim and a perpetrator affect forgiveness? Other Gospel stories about forgiveness have power as an element. The king in Matthew 18 exercised his greater power compassionately in forgiving the steward his debts, and he was then expected to do likewise down the line. There is no indication that Jesus recommended the less powerful to forgive the more powerful. Neither the woman about to be stoned, nor the one with the haemorrhage was told to forgive their tormentors. And Jesus on the cross asked his Father to forgive the crucifiers – he did not announce his own forgiveness.

While there was not time to address gender issues at the workshop, subsequent observation and reading has confirmed that this does indeed need attention. I reviewed a book called *Communicating Forgiveness*[38], a study of forgiveness in mainly long-term relationships. While the two happily married male authors are very positive about forgiveness as a tool for holding all sorts of relationships together, they do acknowledge briefly and at intervals that reconciliation may not be possible or advisable. And:

> We have not studied, and our conclusions do not apply to those who have survived incest, serious crime, domestic violence and other forms of abuse. The process of recovery from these extremely serious transgressions is well beyond the scope of this book.

Following a hunch I totted up on gender lines their often moving anecdotes of forgiveness in relationships. There were twelve stories of men forgiving women partners, and thirty-seven of women forgiving their men. When I asked the authors whether they had noticed this imbalance, no, they had not. But they would give it further thought. Forgiveness is a topic being researched at Arizona State University where the authors are based.

They too identify power issues:

> Individuals who forgive too readily may be maintaining an unhealthy co-dependent relationship with a repeat offender. Low self-esteem and/or low relational power may discourage them from fully confronting wrong-doing. Forgiveness is potentially harmful because the goal is to maintain the relationship at the price of continuing unhealthy patterns of behaviour.

They argue that these approaches are 'a kind of pseudo-forgiveness'.[32] I have heard this sort of comment before from a variety of experts: 'but that's not really forgiveness'. Sadly, this is a subtle distinction that is simply not available to those most intimately concerned, and certainly not one I've ever heard on a Sunday morning.

Domestic violence

A friend who some years ago was being subjected to violence by her husband talked about this in the sacrament of Reconciliation. She was advised, 'Forgive him, go home and try harder to be a good wife.' Not at all OK! Instructions like that and the ministers' statements quoted earlier are what give rise to the Women's Refuge's rather shocking analysis of the Church (generically) as 'an institutional support for battering'. I understand there is now training for clergy on domestic violence. Hopefully this is both mandatory and ongoing.

A prophetic response

Useful in this and other pastoral contexts is the analysis of the Kairos Document (1986).[40] This reflection by a large group of South African church leaders on the then political crisis caused by apartheid contrasts the Christian 'stock ideas' of forgiveness, reconciliation, peace and non-violence, which they call 'church theology', with the need for a 'prophetic theology'. Repeated forgiveness made no impact on the sin of apartheid. So they describe as sin any attempt 'to persuade those of us who are oppressed to accept our oppression and become reconciled to the intolerable crimes committed against us'. And 'like Jesus, we must expose this false peace'. As disciples 'we should promote truth and justice and life at all costs, even at the cost of creating conflict, disunity and dissensions along the way...' (in a domestic context, marriages may break up as a result!):

> If the oppressor does introduce reforms that might lead to real change, this will come about because of a strong pressure from those who are oppressed. True justice, God's justice, demands a radical change of structures. This can only come… from the oppressed themselves.

Oppression is the experience of 'being crushed, degraded, humiliated, exploited, impoverished, defrauded, deceived, enslaved'. Strong words, readily recognizable in the former experience of black South Africans, but how easily do we recognize this as the experience of the woman next door, or of parishioners we sit with on Sunday mornings?

> It cannot be taken for granted' they say, 'that everyone who is oppressed has taken up their own cause and is struggling for their own liberation. Nor can it be assumed that all oppressed Christians are fully aware that their cause is God's cause.… The Church must then help people understand their rights and duties. There must be no misunderstanding about the moral duty of all who are oppressed to resist oppression and to struggle for liberation and justice.

Advice and teaching to simply 'keep on forgiving' does not grow the Shalom of God!

Accountability and justice-seeking

Wellington psychologist Emeritus Professor Tony Taylor published a study called *Justice as a Basic Human Need* (2003).[41] He refers to Maslow's hierarchy of needs and Kohlberg's work on moral development and concludes that claiming and receiving justice can be as important to well-being as other basic life needs. He sees the topic as relevant to psychology, moral philosophy, law and political science. He also mentions the Restorative Justice framework, whose primary aim is to free victims from the effects of the offending.

Taylor's study of justice as a basic human need confirms for me the necessity of inserting 'accountability' between what is usually simplistically presented as the white-black choice between 'forgiveness' and 'revenge and bitterness'. It also connects with Nicola Hoggard-Creegan's paper on the evolutionary roots of sin, where she points out that 'humans and primates share many common proto-moral characteristics'. Perhaps the need for justice has deep evolutionary roots too, similar to the instincts for violence and aggression.

Both writers cite the Restorative Justice framework. This organisation appropriately respects victims' natural timing, the offender often benefits as well, and 'forgiveness' is simply not on the agenda.

Traumatised victims of sin

Judith Hermans in *Trauma and Recovery*[42] warns that encouraging victims of trauma to forgive prematurely is hazardous to their well-being: '… a fantasy of forgiveness … is an attempt at empowerment. The survivor imagines she can transcend her rage and erase the impact of the trauma through a willed defiant act of love. But it is not possible to exorcise the trauma through either hatred or love.'

I get concerned for the long term wellbeing of the families of murder victims who announce that they have forgiven the killers within a day or two of the incident, often to an approving audience of fellow Christians. The normal human healing process is being short-circuited in a probably risky way. If normal and natural emotional responses are suppressed indefinitely the outcomes can predictably be depression and physical illness.

A map

I now hypothesise a dividing line between those victims of injury or damage whose self-hood is relatively intact after the offending, and those whose self-hood has been seriously damaged (then or previously) for the possibly long term future. The first group's personal power may be dented by the offending, but not seriously affected. For them, generously extending forgiveness could eventually be a possible, useful and gracious gift.

But the damaged psyches of the second group will need long, patient and compassionate support and therapy, and some consistent experience of living free from fear to arrive at anything like the liberation and healing promised by Jesus. They can be usefully relieved of the often guilt-inducing burden of struggling unsuccessfully to forgive. The healing route for those 'below the line' is different from that prescribed for those 'above it'. There is a parallel here with quantum physics, where below a certain size particle, a whole different set of rules of behaviour operates, challenging the rules and systems of 'normal' physics.

Teaching for the 'anawim'

I invited a priest to reflect on the impact on a hearer subjected to the on-going violence at home of his Sunday homily statement, 'If they haven't forgotten, they haven't forgiven.' His response was, 'We can't deal to all the hard cases.' However if we truly believe in a God of the marginalised, a God whose preferential option is for the poor, then it is precisely the wellbeing of the 'hard cases' which should have a central position in our reflections and teaching. Their needs and healing matter most when we are offering the Gospel of hope. What in teaching and preaching does them good, and what causes them further harm should be a matter of significant awareness and concern.

Conclusion

So is it really and always wrong to refuse to forgive? Will the God of compassion and healing really refuse to forgive the transgressions of those for whom forgiveness is proving an impossible task? The healing route for some victims of wrong-doing, of sin, is different from the traditionally taught path. Acknowledging and respecting their need to withhold forgiveness could constitute a maturing community theological understanding. If with Irenaeus we believe that, 'The glory of God is a human being fully alive', how can we best assist the damaged ones among us to heal into times of joy? Can moving from simplistic and universal recommendations to forgive, to a greater understanding of the lived experience of traumatised victims mark an increase in pastoral wisdom and usefulness?

I offer these reflections to preachers, pastoral workers and others to invite some going deeper.

2010

Finding Connections

A Religious Studies course at my old university was the locus for this ponder.

A Catholic Charismatic Prayer Group, Wellington, NZ, and the Healing Dance of the !Kung of the Kalahari Desert

When in the mid 1970s I was taught a new way to pray, and thence to pray for healing for others with laying on of hands, I had no idea that I was being inducted into a ritual that could be as old as the human race itself. None of us had. We only knew this Way was old: it had almost 2000 years of Christian history. We understood the release of the Holy Spirit of God in our lives as accessing the same experience that the disciples of Jesus had at Pentecost. It got them past their fear. It empowered them to preach, heal and understand other languages. Baptism in the Holy Spirit was simply taking possession of our heritage as Catholic Christians, the fullness of what Jesus had come to impart. I was involved with that prayer group until the late 1980s. It certainly had a formative effect on my faith and life. Understanding it as part of a much longer story came very much later.

Then thirty years on from my initial charismatic experience, I read about the !Kung[43] people of the Kalahari Desert, and their spiritual beliefs and practices. They are hunter-gatherers, a way of life that goes back to the earliest human history. As I worked through the reading[44] about their healing dance my hair started to stand on end as I realised how many elements of !Kung ritual experience were familiar to me from my prayer group days. And when I saw the video clip[45] of their healing dance this was reinforced visually: 'I've been there, I've done that, that's what we used to do!'

Despite the extraordinary differences between the surroundings, cultures and understanding of God/gods of Kalahari bush people and a suburban Christian prayer group, here, in a summary of statements from Richard Katz's report, are some of the similar dynamics I recognized from prayer group days:

!Kung share material resources, and have an egalitarian society with no 'special' people. The life of the spirit is an inextricable aspect of everyday life and religion is simply their way of living. They pray as individuals speaking directly to the gods at any time it feels necessary. The healing activities and rituals seek health and growth on physical, psychological, social and spiritual levels. Becoming a healer is normal, not reserved for a few persons with unique characteristics or extraordinary powers. Kia seems to be an altered state of consciousness verging on transcendence. During their non-kia state, the teachers/healers remain ordinary persons. They do not demand of students either obedience or a long apprenticeship - the emphasis is on experiential education. Their healing approach deals with the whole person, in all aspects and situations.

'Num' is an energy held in awe and considered very powerful and mysterious, which though originally from the gods, regularly passes from person to person. Num is not 'put into' someone who cannot accept it: students must be willing and ready to receive the num which can then evoke the experience of 'kia.' They do not seek num for its own sake – it is to provide protection and growth for the individual, the group and the culture simultaneously. The community both heals and is healed. Num does not reverse a situation which is supposed to be.

The students are socialised to expect and seek kia, and must give up their familiar identity to enter the potentially frightening unknown territory. When potential healers can willingly let this 'die', the fear of num can be overcome, and there can be a breakthrough to kia. The anticipation of being reborn or coming alive again is useful. The teacher, perhaps with one or two other healers, will probably be the one who tries to invoke num into a student during a dance. They then experience themselves as living beyond the ordinary level by becoming more essential, more themselves. The !Kung are clear about what happens during kia, and its experiential mystery.

The Giraffe dance is a point of marked intensity and significance in their daily lives. It provides healers with opportunities for fulfilment and growth, where all can experience a sense of wellbeing, and some a spiritual development. The entire community participates and offers support by their presence. As the mood intensifies, the singing and clapping become more spirited, the dancing more focussed, and they stimulate the num 'to boil'. One person going into kia is usually a stimulant for others.

They believe specific illnesses are a sign of some imbalance in the whole individual as they exist in their total environment. The healers lay their fluttering hands on a person, pulling out the sickness, then they shake their hands vigorously toward the empty space beyond the dance, casting the sickness they have taken from the person out into the darkness. Cures can be 'dramatic' or 'undramatic'. The one being healed can also die, and a new balance still be established. They integrate elements from other treatment systems into their dance. After spending the night in the intense intimacy of the healing dance, they talk of how good it is to be together.

If one replaces 'num' with 'the Holy Spirit', then the dynamics of the prayer group and the Life in the Spirit Seminar were very similar to those of the !Kung healing dance. 'Kia' seems to equate to the felt manifestation of Spirit 'using the gifts of the Spirit', those less ordinary ones of healing, prophecy, tongues, words of knowledge and others. At the prayer group there wasn't exactly a dance, but certainly a lot more physical expression than is encountered in the average Sunday congregation – clapping, singing, raising the arms, laying on of hands for healing prayer and sometimes uncontrollable shaking.

The clincher for me in this déjà vu experience was the report that !Kung healers shake their hands outside the healing circle 'casting the sickness they have taken from the person out into the darkness'. I was taught to make this very same gesture for the very same reason. That is when the connection really hit home! Are these religious practices from the same ancient root? Did slaves take the practices from Africa to the New World whence it became part of the Christianised Negro spirituality, and thus into Pentecostalism? Or has there been some more recent cross-pollination? Or, as someone later suggested, do they all spring from the same Jungian collective unconscious?

And then a semantic connection: the very word num sounds so foreign and unconnected with anything we have ever heard. But the next time I came across the word numinous, I leapt from my chair with shock and excitement and took my ancient Latin dictionary from its shelf. Numen, as it then confirmed, does indeed mean 'the divine will, power of the gods, divine sway, supreme authority', then later 'divinity, deity, god, goddess'. Could this word have worked its way down Africa from days when North Africa was part of the Roman Empire: Carthage was destroyed by Roman legions in 148BCE. Or do numen and the !Kung num have a common Sanskrit root?

To discover the similarities in ritual between !Kung and prayer group has opened a whole new series of possible understandings about the primal roots of Christian worship. Other than being very sure all this is not a coincidence, there are lots of questions, mostly without answers, but still worth the asking!

2006

Shamans and Mystics

Fifteen years ago I was astounded and inspired by the writings of British monk Bede Griffiths[46] on the common ground between the Hindu faith and Christianity. It had never occurred to me that there was any – quite the opposite in fact! I'd learned that monotheism really was 'right' and polytheism really was 'wrong'. Then there was Thomas Merton and his respectful appreciation of Buddhism. Another major interfaith bridge! These two gave me a tool for engaging with another not-Christian spirituality.

> Seeing ever more clearly how different faiths are essentially different metaphor systems describing similar Realities.

Eco-spirituality has become something of a buzz word in the church, and rightly so. It is also good to acknowledge that Christianity has come to this understanding quite late in the day. The Shamanic framework goes back to the early days of the human race, well before the arrival of the five patriarchal religions. It has been preserved largely by indigenous people – Māori tohunga, North American Indian medicine men and women, Aboriginal ngangkari, Celtic, Tibetan and other shamans. These are the ones who are the contact with the world of spirit on behalf of their people. They all have been deeply immersed in the natural world for the centuries when westerners were mostly caught up in scientific rationalism and the domination of the earth and its other forms of life.

Modern Shamanic teaching has drawn on indigenous knowledge with respect and appreciation and is being made available through literature and workshops to a wide range of interested learners. It is beneficent in intent. I attended a workshop in an isolated corner of Marlborough Sounds offered by Dr John Broomfield and his wife Jo Imlay. Again it was a book that had sparked the interest: John's *Other Ways of Knowing*[47] had also made a deep impression a few years previously. It gathered up a lot of my learning and extended it in often challenging directions. Interspecies communication was one!

He told a story of Jo's communication with some bothersome wasps. She realised they were thirsty and put out sugar water for them. Not only did they settle down, but in time they even came to let her know when more was needed. Suddenly the recognition of Francis of Assisi as a shaman! He talked to the wild creatures too. And the story of the wolf of Gubbio morphed from 'medieval legend' to 'this could have literally true!'

Shamans often come into their power after a severe illness or trauma. In the Christian mystical tradition many of the saints had this experience – Julian of Norwich, Ignatius, Hildegard and others. They 'came back' and told us what they had experienced and learned in that other realm. It was their gift to the wider church and community. And Christian priesthood is at one level about mediating connection with the spiritual world, knowledge and healing.

Shamanic terminology is different, but the experiences and their fruits are often the same as those of Christian prayer traditions. They talk of spirit guides – and that is exactly the role Jesus holds for the Christian: teacher, guide, intermediary. Someone to spend time with, to seek help from. And then there are the power animals. While at first this seemed very different from Christian thinking, eventually I understood the concept as another set of metaphors for what we might call guardian angels. And images/imaginings of God as mother eagle and mother bear, or Jesus comparing himself to a mother hen are straight from Scripture – we just haven't called them power animals!

The contemplative exercises inviting us to engage with an aspect of the natural world that we were given at the workshop could have come straight from a Catholic retreat. Thirty years ago at one retreat we were offered a tray of flowers, invited to choose one, spend time with it and see what it had to say to us. On that occasion a daphne sprig had a great deal to say to me about the nature of community!

What Shamanic tradition would call trance, Christians would call deep prayer. Both are a way to seek for truth, guidance and deep healing. What they call visiting the Land of the Dead, we would again call prayer. At another retreat my director suggested going with Jesus to meet a dead family member. The encounter that ensued was dramatic and healing. What they call the 'retrieval of soul fragments', we would call 'healing of memories'. And so it went on, with the focus on Spirit, who is to be found everywhere in everything, and willing and ready to communicate guidance, wisdom and love. And so to a reverence for life that extends to all creation. I recognise our God and what the Christian tradition would call panentheism, the supreme Spirit in and through everything. We are about the same stuff!

Modern western-flavoured shamanic teaching might be seen as imitative of indigenous knowledge and so perhaps a colonising, but this is an incomplete perspective. The white people who have been admitted to the sacred knowledge of indigenous people have approached it with the utmost respect, and have earned the respect of the people concerned. But shamanism is indeed in our own ancestry and heritage as well, but was frowned on by the church that saw all other spiritualities as 'wrong' and 'dangerous'. So it was virtually wiped out and abandoned along with the deep connection to the earth and its other living beings. We don't have to go back very far to find our own ancestry immersed in this ancient tradition, particularly if we have Celtic blood in us.

So this was an enriching week that joined yet more dots for me in the realisation that so many spiritual paths converge. Those who engage with Spirit, Life and Earth, and seek the good of all are truly pilgrim companions on the Way. We are all called to be mystics! Different traditions hand on the same essential wisdom – Seek! Look! Listen!

• • •

> Shamanism is an age old practice of entering into an altered state of consciousness with the purpose of journeying in spirit realms to seek knowledge and healing. Shamanism rests on a belief that all of nature is conscious and inspirited and that human health – the health of individuals and whole communities – depends on a harmonious balance with nature. The maintenance of that balance is the work of shamans, talented individuals who have mastered the techniques of journeying and who have established powerful connections with spirit helpers.
> *Dr John Broomfield eagle@ts.co.nz*

2009

The M-Word

A group of five women counsellors were having a Christmas meal together in a restaurant, among a dozen other groups of people doing likewise. The conversation casually ranged over what we were going to do for Christmas Day, our work loads, the day's weather, what we'd done since last being together... then just as casually turned to masturbation. Casually, that is, for three of the five. The other two of us, the cradle Catholics, sort of froze, salmon fettucine half way to mouths. **Talking** about it! **Here?** In public? Like it didn't matter, and was no more significant than any other socially acceptable human activity? We eventually acknowledged our discomfort. 'But why?' said the others, somewhat mystified. They knew Catholics had odd ideas about a lot of things. Here was one more. Amazing what prompts theological reflection! How come it was a matter of little or no concern to our friends, and the conversation for us was an almost heart-stopping breaking of a very old taboo? 'Why?' indeed! So I embarked on a tour of sources and stories in an effort to discover the 'why'.

> A self-explanatory piece of theological enquiry.

First stop: Church literature. The Catholic Catechism[48] pronounces the said activity to be 'an intrinsically and gravely disordered action.' 'The deliberate use of the sexual faculty for any reason whatsoever outside marriage is essentially contrary to its purpose.' 'For here sexual pleasure is sought outside of the sexual relationship which is demanded by the moral order and in which the total meaning of mutual self-giving and human procreation in the context of true love is achieved.'

Another compendium of the faith says masturbation is sinful, because if indulged in, it might become addictive, and thus impede the formation of healthy relationships. It struck me that there is no comparable dictum about drinking alcohol – far more likely, in my opinion, to be followed by those dire predictions! Is that really what the old hellfire and brimstone prohibitions are based on? With the attendent threats of 'You'll go blind' (possibly shades of Sodom from Genesis 19,11) 'You'll go mad' etc. Though apparently those predictions are more likely related to the 17th century scientific belief that it was the excessive expenditure of sexual energy which produced those very symptoms. The discovery of syphilis and the actual mode of transmission by contact with an infected party was still a couple of hundred years into the future. A case of misinterpretation and misconnection!

Second Stop: Sex researchers. In the early years of the 20th century, Hirschfield (Germany) assessed that 96% of under 20s had masturbated and concluded that exaggerated fear of the consequences was more harmful than the act itself. Havelock-Ellis (England) coined the term auto-eroticism – he saw the term 'self-abuse' as a psychological killer. He wanted 'to transform the activity from a malignant vice to a benign inevitability'. The more recent term self-pleasuring takes this process even further[49]. A vaguely remembered 1980s article on psycho-sexual development by Father Richard Rohr OFM listed nine stages of development, and he said that omitting any of these stages will at some point stifle mature development. There will be a need to go back and remedy the situation. Masturbation appears as one of the earlier stages of growth. Question: if God has actually designed human beings to develop in this way, is it OK, necessary even, to respect the normal, natural progression towards becoming a fully alive, sexually mature individual?

Third Stop: *Courage to Heal*[50], a book that thousands of women have found to be Good News ('Gospel') as they travel the rocky journey of healing from sexual abuse. Authors Ellen Bass and Laura Davis say that masturbation is a good way to become reconnected with one's own body in a non-threatening situation. They quote a woman survivor as saying 'If I can't have sex with myself there's no point in trying to do it with anyone else.' Learning therapeutic self-touch and physical awareness can be a valuable means of over-coming dissociation and fear. They affirm bodies as being 'rich and marvellous'. 'Sex is about connection', they say, 'in this case, your connection with yourself.'

Fourth Stop: Memories of a conversation at a spiritual directors' meeting about sexual arousal and masturbation during prayer. This is not something that one hears about from the pulpit on a Sunday morning. Not surprising, really. But mystics, known and canonised like John of the Cross and Teresa of Avila, and unknown, usually startled, often scared, ordinary pray-ers have acknowledged passionate love affairs with their God. Is it really so shocking or astonishing if a spiritual love encompasses the whole being? Spirituality and sexuality are increasingly recognised as two sides of the same coin – the essence of our identity, the core of who we are.

Fifth Stop: memories of now-ex-Father Felix Donnelly confronting the Church with his conclusions on this topic in the 1970s and 80s, with the conviction of a prophet who had read the signs, saying 'You have got it wrong!' Now we know, if we have read our bibles, what happens to prophets. And so it did.

Counsellors and spiritual directors (*and confessors?*) still see people who are crippled with guilt about their 'sin'. They know (*or do they?*) that guilt and a frontal (whoops!) attack on any compulsion are likely to compound the problem. Non-judgemental, gentle acceptance will probably allow it to resolve eventually. And anyway, if it weren't for the Church-imposed guilt, is the problem really a problem? Or does it become so only through the teaching of the Church?

Which way does the life-giving compass needle point? A grave sin? – or a normal and necessary part of human growth and experience? With possibilities, even, of sacredness, healing, and gratitude for the gift of our sexual selves? Having explored some of our stories, searched in vain for specific scriptural condemnations, and using the powers of reason available to me, I would now vote for the latter position. Maybe at the next gathering with my friends I will be able to recount my voyage of exploration in a search for the answer to their 'Why?' No longer will I feel I am indulging in some heretical sinful deviance by discussing the ordinary stuff of human experience!

1996

Expanding the Metaphors: Validating Feminine Images of God [51]

This was my contribution to the Catholic Institute of Theology book on speaking about God today.

I write as a voice from the outside: outside the academic framework, and outside the institutional Church whose language eventually made it impossible for me to remain. This is for me a place of freedom and choices. My shared life with other writers is the God/Jesus who has been central to my existence since I was little, a passion for the power of language, and a passion that the Church should by the language it uses facilitate people's responding to Divine Love, which is after all its primary role. I describe myself as feminist thealogian, and these days as a hermit.

I look at the sources of our metaphors for God, share images from my reading and listening, point to women's need to image the Divine as feminine, look at the implications for ministry, and conclude that where there is a strong correlation between communal metaphors and those potent ones that arise from within the psyche, the Good News will be more easily heard and received.

Traditional Church Imaging of God

The way human beings understand, image and name the Divine has enormous implications for our spiritual, emotional, mental and social health. Those of us who have grown in faith within the Judaeo-Christian tradition were given by our Scriptures, creeds and liturgies a very clear idea of who God is, what God is like, how to please God, what God will do for us. For most this has meant images that include a Heavenly Father who created all from nothing, who is omniscient, omnipotent, all-loving, which somehow fits with His punishing the bad and rewarding the good. It goes without saying that this God is male. Or rather, the way of the 'saying' has made this very clear.

Many people of faith in recent years have been questioning whether these images of God are in fact universally useful in this third millennium. I believe 'Church-speak,' is indeed confining, even impeding the spiritual growth of many people. A few years ago I was asked by a young man from an evangelical church 'Are you a Christian?' 'It depends what you mean by Christian', I replied cautiously. If he'd said 'Do you lead a Christ-centred life?' he'd have got an immediate 'That's what I aim for!' But no: his response was to ask 'Do you believe that God the Father sent Jesus to die for our sins?' I pondered deeply before replying 'No, I don't think I do'. Naming God as Father was indeed one significant part of the problem.

All is Metaphor

Augustine is reputed to have said that if we think we have understood God, what we have understood is not God. That is certainly an urging to broaden our horizons when thinking and speaking of the Divine. Metaphor is 'the application of name or descriptive term to an object to which it is not literally applicable.' Discovering Thomas Aquinas' saying that 'all language about God is analogy'[52] was for me a freeing delight. This immediately deliteralises the standard God-words. *All* our words for God, as with any metaphor, are saying 'there are ways in which God is like this', but they can never fully contain the Infinite, nor can they be mutually exclusive. When we acknowledge the ineffable, beyond-anything-we-can-understand nature of the Divine, how true this seems!

I can assume readers' familiarity with the male and non-human Scriptural metaphors for the Divine. Also with those of the Divine as Mother Eagle (Deut 32:10-12), Mother Bear (Hosea 13:8) Mother Hen (Matthew 23:37), as Baker-woman (Matthew 13:33), and a pregnant (Deut 32:18) or nursing mother (Isaiah 49:15). Sadly these feminine images have been systematically excluded from the communal liturgical Christian expression of faith for most of its existence. This centuries-old exclusion both drew from and reinforced the prevailing patriarchal cultures.

Our God images, healthy or otherwise, are formed not just by Scripture and liturgy, but also by our early life experiences, especially with our fathers, because of the constant use of the Father image of God in the liturgy. Is there a discrepancy between faith ('God loves me') and the actual experience of and relating to the Divine? Harmful images of God can be based unconsciously on the experience of intolerant and demanding fathers. There are many people burdened by such images.

Many of the good people who give up on God and church seem to me to be not 'losing their faith', but rightly and honestly protesting against the imposition of God-images which are not life-giving for them. Sadly, this is often reinforced when the Church, by word, deed or omission, gives God a bad name at critical moments in people's lives. Their gut tells them that to be of any use, a 'real' God would have to be experienced as loving, as life-giving. To know a loving and life-giving God is the birthright of God's people. Ministers who have some deepened understanding of this are going to be experienced as loving, and hopefully offer a window through which the God who really cares can be met.

New Words for God

How are people experiencing Divine Love these days? There are beautiful images that theologians, the truth-seekers, have offered us:

'Ground of our Being'[53]

'Life-giver, Pain-Bearer, Love-Maker[54]

God as 'Verb'[55]

'Mother Sophia'[56]

'God is simply, cosmically, and prophetically the spirit of hospitality itself'[57]

Here are three more namings that have recently fed my spirit. Marcella Althaus Reid (Professor of Theology, Edinburgh University) speaks of 'Queer God', the God who does not 'keep the rules', who 'queers the pitch', who champions the poor, marginalised and dispossessed, and yes, there are the sexual connotations as well[58]. Philip Culbertson and Tavita Maliko look at the Pacific Island traditions of a 'third gender' (fa'afafine in Samoan): 'If we could push further apart the gendered metaphors we ordinarily use for God, what might we find in 'the marginalized center'? What could we understand of God if we spoke metaphorically of the Divine *Fa'afafine* who inhabits liminal spaces, rather than of Father Lord and Mother God?'[59] Then cosmologist Brian Swimme's amazing phrase All-Nourishing Abyss.[60] This is what astrophysicists have discovered must exist to constantly generate and re-generate the totality of What Is! I equate this to 'God', the One who originates, permeates and sustains.

Words from other Traditions

Seeing all naming of God as metaphor opens a door to appreciation of and enrichment by non-traditional namings, and those of other traditions. Elizabeth Johnson has gathered in her book on God such beautiful Jewish names from the 1st- 4th centuries CE as Friend of the World and Searcher of Hearts; and African namings including Architect of the World, Great Mother.[61] And there's Edwina Gateley's Warm Moist Salty God, also from Africa[62]. Islam has its 99 deep names for God, and the hundredth is silence.

Recognising God

With other spiritual directors, I understand God as already operating in many guises and disguises: in an atheist's awe at a mountain sunset, in the experience of 'being in another dimension' that musicians can have, in community as it is lived in many so-called 'secular' settings, in the soft purple rug that comforts an abuse victim. The key question: is the experience or image life-giving? If so, God is there! It is through people's own healing and awe-provoking images that God can both work and be experienced as Love.

All is sacred!

Three stories from my immediate network:

A friend's three year old grand-daughter was talking about Christmas, and suddenly announced 'Jesus should have been a girl'. Grandma, intrigued, asked 'Why do you say that?' 'Because' replied the small one immediately, '*I'm* a girl!'

An elderly Christian intellectual expressed his unease with the concept of a feminine image of God, because, he said, 'If God was feminine, I'd lose my identity!'

An 88 year-old Catholic woman, a life-long pray-er, confessed very diffidently that she could no longer say 'Glory be to the Father…' When encouraged to elaborate, she said 'Now I have to say 'Glory be to the Source of All Things…'

What is going on here? For all three people there is a need to be able to do their own naming of God because of its deep impact on their own identity. The man seems to have no awareness of what the reverse situation might be like for women who just as innately need to claim some identity with the Divine. And the innocence of the young and wisdom of the old point to a feminine instinct away from naming God as masculine that has long been denied in church discourse.

Gender-Neutral Images of God

In June 2007 I spent four days in Whanganui with a group of 26 Quakers, men and women, at a workshop called Metaphors of Meaning. Because their communal worship is in silence, and individual journeys are highly valued, there are no metaphors that are liturgically or organisationally imposed around religious beliefs and experiences. This workshop/retreat was a time to explore our own and each others' language for the Divine to see whether there were common threads.

There was a unanimous rejection of the images of Father, King, Lord and Shepherd as being unhelpful and inappropriate to their non-hierarchic culture and philosophy. There was a strong identification with words like Light, Water, Breath, Food, Fire and Spirit. These are universal and timeless human experiences of the Divine, based on the meeting of our fundamental human needs. They also appear in Scripture. The closest to a communal Quaker understanding would be the term Inner Light, from the writings of George Fox and used to denote what other Christians might call the indwelling Holy Spirit. The phrase 'I'll hold you in the Light' is a beautiful equivalent to 'I will pray for you'.

Other non-gendered words such as Source, Energy, Wellspring, and Presence (which is increasingly used in trans-faith writing) can open hearts to new experiences and understandings of God. And there are of course the other familiar scriptural images: Rock, Shelter, Breeze and others.

Towards Feminine Images of God

Because of how life has been, I, along with countless other women, eventually found the virtually exclusive naming of the Divine as male in Christian culture and liturgies not simply intellectually distasteful, but deeply and physically painful. Being able to say 'God… She' was a release. When this becomes one's natural mode of naming, it makes remaining committed to Sunday mass very difficult. Have you ever counted the number of times 'Father', 'Lord' and 'He' appear in the standard Sunday liturgy, starting with the initial sign of the cross? Try fifty or more! I have been heartsick as yet another generation of little girls learns by subliminal Sunday osmosis that their fathers and brothers are like God in a way they cannot ever match.

I – we – have found we need a God who knows what it is like to be Woman! Admittedly, this too is only part of the story. When some years ago I shared my perspective with my parish priest, he rightly pointed out that simply giving God a feminine 'identity' and naming is as inaccurate as using the traditional masculine. I wasn't quick enough that day to reply 'True, but why use one inaccuracy 99.9% of the time?' That is working on the intellectual level.

But then there is Jung: we human beings of both genders, need to integrate both female and male elements (anima, animus) within our psyche. Without both, balance is missing. This too has something to do with God. What if, for their most profound identification with and relationship to both their own anima and the Divine, women need innately to image God primarily as feminine like themselves? Just as much as men, including the fully human Jesus, need to image God as masculine like themselves? What of the men who need to image God as feminine?

Some shifts have occurred in New Zealand across the denominations in the last 20 or so years. Back then I heard a priest in his Sunday homily speak of the universe as being 'in the womb of God'. My response was one of shocked delight! Many ministers in less traditional Presbyterian and Methodist parishes use 'God… She'. Many Catholic Sisters do likewise. Using the spelling 'Godde' is also fairly common among Christian women, locating the Divine a tad closer to Goddess than to the familiar perceived-as-male 'God'.

Women are saying…
From her research on images of God among mid-life Catholic women, Mary Betz reported them in 2005[63] as describing God thus:

> [She] was deeply present, close, yet bigger than anyone could fathom… the painter of sunsets, creator of opportunity, … in the ever-changing light over the sea: in-dwelling in each person and in relationships… a feminine presence, a well of love, nurturer; continually enfolding, empowering towards freedom; birth-giver…; in the storm which stirs up the depths, calling us to growth.

How dynamic! How freeing! How frustrating the block at institutional level which keeps most of these beautiful life-giving images out of the formal words of the liturgy! The Vatican in various instructions from the Congregation for the Doctrine of the Faith since Vatican II has consistently said no feminine words or images for God should be used in the prayers of the mass. And in 2011 it declared that even gender neutral words like Creator, Redeemer, Sanctifier invalidate the sacramental liturgy of baptism.[64]

It is intriguing that non-church, non-Christian women are using very similar terminology for the Divine. These words describing the Goddess are from a New Zealand woman who identified herself as a witch:

> At times I think of [Her] as my real self; it's the real me becoming balanced and whole. At times it's all of nature; …at times it's just what I'm needing when I don't feel I have a lot inside. I want to think of a symbol outside myself and so I think of [Her] outside myself. So it's outside, and within, and through the whole of creation. … always loving and caring and supportive

and helping me to get back to a centre of balance. …. You are linking with every other person's idea of [Her] too… the Universal Consciousness.[65]

And from US thealogian and process philosopher Carol P. Christ[66] who in a recent book uses the configuration 'Goddess/God' to name the Divine:

To be open to Goddess/God is to be open to the whole world and its deepest meaning. …a sense of inner knowing that I am alive, embodied, and embedded in a changing web of life and relationships co-created by myself, other individuals, and Goddess/God whose love supports and sustains the world…

There is an underground river of women's spirituality emerging from the depths after 5000 years or so of suppression by patriarchal religions. It is happening both within and beyond the churches, but the similarities of expressions in these various streams are too close to be ignored. The Divine Feminine is awakening the world with new hope for peace, respect for other human beings, the rest of life, our beautiful planet and the entire universe. God is manifesting as She chooses! Can the Christian Church respond to the invitation to enrich itself and all its people by giving equal value to the ancient and new feminine images of the Divine, of God?

There are the communally imposed or taught metaphors, appropriate – or not – to the hearers, and there are the metaphors that emerge from within individual souls. I believe that those that are generated by each human person are those which are most effective in connecting them with the Divine. Where many are generating similar metaphors, the Church could usefully listen. Vox mulierium[67] vox Dei!

Inculturation

Then the inculturation concept: those in 'mission' work understand the need to use the language, symbol and metaphor system of a people if the core Christian message is to be wholeheartedly received. They know the power of metaphor is generated by culture and context.

When Bishop Bob Leamy was consecrated as Bishop of the Cook Islands in 1984, he was not presented with the traditional crozier because the lack of sheep on the islands rendered the 'shepherding' symbol irrelevant. He received a ceremonial paddle to symbolise that he would be the steersman of their canoe of faith – a beautiful example of inculturation! And in many Māori Catholic churches the tabernacle is constructed as a pataka, the traditional storehouse for food. So right!

What would inculturation mean for the tribe of women? What if *our* language/culture/symbols/metaphor system were to be consciously adopted to preach the Good News to us, so that we too could understand more deeply, more immediately, that we are made in God's image? This would necessarily mean putting our birthing and bleeding and feeding experiences alongside those already at the heart of Crucifixion/Eucharist. For these to be overtly acknowledged in the regular liturgies, where we make up a large proportion of the numbers, would take something of a miracle! But there has to be hope!

Decolonisation

Decolonisation has been an important strand of recent thinking in Aotearoa New Zealand. With developing awareness in many countries over the last thirty or so years, much progress has been made in acknowledging the rights of indigenous peoples to their own governance, language, spiritual understandings and social customs. And while we have by no means got it all right yet, there are few countries where the level of recognition for their voices is as accepted as it is here. It is now acknowledged that the right to retain their names for geographic features was removed from Māori by British colonisers in the 19th century. Taranaki became Mt Egmont. Recent more respectful and just attitudes have meant the 'allowing' again of the Māori right to name. So Taranaki and other places are once more proudly wearing their original and rightful names. This has been about tangata whenua reclaiming the right to name as it fits for them, and official recognition that this right should be restored, validated and legitimised. What if women's right to name the God of their experience were again officially accepted? Who would lose? What would be lost? And decolonisation goes way beyond simply restoring naming rights!

Just doing it

What if women simply go ahead and do what they need to do? In November 2007, I attended a conference at a Lutheran parish in San Francisco called *herchurch*[68], where women and men use feminine images of God in the Sunday liturgy and elsewhere. Goddess and God are interchangeable names, the writings of women are used in the liturgy, and a beautiful Eucharistic prayer honouring women as the growers of the wheat and makers of the bread precedes the words of blessing. Hymns are sung to Mother Eagle and Divine Midwife[69]. It was a deeply joyful and freeing experience to worship in my own 'language'. The conference, *Wisdom's Urgent Cry*, looked at the challenge to the Churches of feminine imagery for the Divine. Keynote speaker Dr Jann Aldredge-Clanton connected exclusive male imagery for God with the globally pervasive oppression of women and their poverty[70]. She proposes Christ- Sophia as gender-inclusive name for the post-resurrection Jesus[71].

Change is Possible

Can we supplement our current images of the Divine with the wonderful kaleidoscope we have on offer today? Who does Goddess/God want to be for me? For you? For the Christian tradition as expressed in the churches? Perhaps we dare say to Goddess/God 'How shall we newly name you?' And how can we more deeply comprehend the old image whose depths are never fully plumbed – God is Love? People are so hungry for love and acceptance. How can the Church more effectively use its formal language to share this Good News?

Implications for Ministry

For those of us who minister: I believe it is crucial to own the images of God we have ourselves internalised, to have some sense where they came from, what they bring of healing or harm, and why they are the ones we choose to retain. And are we able to engage respectfully with the images of God of those to whom we minister? Are we able to help them discern the helpfulness or otherwise of their images to their relationship with the Divine?

It would be sublimely sensitive if ministers of the Gospel could enquire about the images of God that are relevant to those to whom they minister, and not make assumptions from their own vocabulary and experience. Questions like 'How do you see/imagine God?', 'What words do you have for your God?', and 'How would you like me to pray for/with you?' If as a minister I am to wash someone's feet, I move from my own comfortable ground to kneel reverently on the ground that he/she occupies. Apply this verbally: if someone who is being ministered to can only relate to God as feminine, it is a hurtful violation to impose a 'Heavenly Father' and 'God ... He'. This applies equally, of course, in the other direction: when I am working with those who use traditional male words for God, in love I use their language for the sake of their peace. Not that it is easy, but it must be done!

Conclusion

While theologically it is acknowledged that God is beyond gender, I believe the thoughtless use of one deficient set of gendered words virtually all the time is insupportable, even if the other set is equally inadequate. To quote Fr Neil Darragh 'The Church can no longer use male God-language in innocence'. Where there is a strong correlation between communally used metaphors and those potent ones that arise from within the psyche, the Good News will be heard and received at a deeper level by women. The dream I have for the Church is that both feminine and masculine metaphors for Goddess/God will be equally acknowledged and articulated: Mother and Father, Sophia and Logos, Papatūānuku (Earth Mother) and Rangi (Sky Father). *Not* two Gods, but two equally valued images of God, two metaphors for the Divine!

Mary and Me

We've come a long way through many winding paths, but there she is on the new shelf in my bedroom, smooth, red (matching the velvet curtains) and holding that Baby. And she's in my lounge too, a beautiful cream German porcelain statue, with a book and the Baby, now a toddler, standing on her knee. I don't remember where the red figure came from, but the cream one has a story. It was in the recycling shop at the local landfill, filthy dirty, must have been in someone's garage for twenty years or more. No-one on Trademe had wanted her. I didn't really either. But no mother deserves that sort of neglect, so I took her home, gave her a very good scrub, and a place of honour on my woman-altar. A friend who is spiritually aware said 'I think there's something symbolic going on here!' A couple of years down the track, I think I agree.

Since the Crete journey, I've lived with the question 'How could Mary possibly be Goddess?' A review of my evolving relationship with her has had its own interest.

In my young days in the north of England, our wonderful curate who nurtured my child-faith got me interested in Mary. If I learned all the dates of her feastdays, he'd give me a book. An irresistible bait! So I did, and in those days there were at least twenty of them! The book was the story of her Fatima apparitions, and I didn't at all think it was fair that those children had such a rotten time with lots of people being mean to them, then two of them dying of influenza, and the third left with the huge and mysterious secret. I was very glad Mary didn't appear to me!

What I did enjoy was 'her' special month of May, and the May processions from school the few hundred yards to the church. We were all in our white dresses and veils, with baskets of rose petals to be strewn along the footpath ahead of her statue, which rode on a bier carried by some of the older boys. One of the older girls had been chosen to be the May Queen and have the privilege of placing the coronet of flowers on the statue once we'd reached the church. And all the Protestants came to watch. It felt like there was safety in Catholic numbers, and that they were all quite envious that their church didn't do lovely things like this. And we sang words that I loved:

> Bring flowers the rarest, bring flowers the fairest
> From garden and woodland and hillside and vale;
> Our full hearts are swelling, our glad voices telling
> The praise of the loveliest Rose of the vale.

> *Refrain:*
> Oh Mary, we crown you with blossoms today,
> Queen of the Angels, Queen of the May.
> Our voices ascending, in harmony blending,
> Oh, thus may our hearts turn, dear Mother, to you.
> Oh, thus shall we prove you how truly we love you;
> How dark without Mary life's journey would be.[22]

No thoughts crossed my mind then of any connection with the pre-Christian fertility symbol maypole and its ribbon dances at the school up the road, or the goddesses Flora and Maya whom I'd met in my book of Roman mythology. Why would they? We were Catholics in a Protestant land and Mary was ours, Jesus too!

When I was at the state secondary school in Tauranga, New Zealand in the 1950s I belonged to the Children of Mary and the Legion of Mary. It was in the days of parish sodalities – holy clubs, the precursors in a way to lay ministry. They were what you did if your Sunday Mass attendance wasn't 'enough'. The children of Mary were the chaste (mostly, most of the time) young women of the parish. Once a month we gathered at the parish mass wearing our blue cloaks and veils to show our intentions and devotion. And all the greater was the scandal if a Child of Mary got pregnant! The Legion was different, with terminology based on the organization of the army of classical Rome. Men and women belonged and did good works. Again the words were potent for me:

> Who is she that comes forth as the morning rising, fair as the moon, bright as the sun, terrible as an army set in battle array?

But in the end spiritual warfare wasn't my thing. We were still too close to the war of my childhood for it to grab me as a concept or motivator. My Queen of Heaven was all for peace!

Mary faded from my view until I had my own children. I wondered then how she'd coped with sleepless nights, or maybe the Perfect Child simply didn't have colic or teething problems. And my friends and I felt a bit cynical about the Holy Family as role models for common or garden parents like ourselves.

After Vatican II, I realized that seeing her as a woman of faith, a 3-D human being made a lot of sense, and that some of her beautiful titles in the Litany I loved – more words – really belonged to the Holy Spirit.

> Mirror of justice, Seat of Wisdom, Cause of our joy, Spiritual vessel, Vessel of honour, Singular vessel of devotion, Mystical rose, Tower of David, Tower of ivory, House of gold, Ark of the Covenant, Gate of Heaven, Morning star…

When, in the community I belonged to through the 1980s, the concept of male headship became current, being subject to one's husband just didn't make sense to me. Mary had not told the visiting Gabriel 'Just a minute while I go and ask Joseph'. She made the decision herself to put her own life on the line for this Child. Good enough for me!

Then, along with other women I knew from church, I began to question the concept of virginity as a mark of sanctity. Married love was not and had rarely ever been prized as a sacred gift of God. We couldn't model ourselves on someone who was reputedly a virgin. About then a nun asked how it would affect my faith if Mary wasn't a virgin. With a surge of joy, I realized it would be strengthened rather than anything. And I got pretty angry with the idea that the church Fathers at the Council of Ephesus in 431 AD had sat round discussing the state of Mary's hymen during the birth of Jesus. It seemed appallingly intrusive and abusive!

Some years later again, I was pondering the nature of priesthood and the banning by John Paul II of any discussion of the ordination of women. It occurred to me that Mary was the first real priest of the Christian tradition. She received Jesus as a gift from God, made him available to the community of the world, and ultimately on Calvary (as I understood it then) offered him back to his Father. Surely that was the essence of priesthood. Surely she was a priest!

I tried this out on a good Marist priest, expecting him to see this too. Marists were deeply imbued with devotion to and understanding of the Woman. But: 'Someone painted Mary in priestly vestments back in the 1950s and the pope banned it.' End of conversation. I soon discovered that Mechthild of Magdeburg had had a vision of Mary in priestly vestments back in the 13th century. Women have been thinking about these things for a long time. Another whose reflections have taken her down this track is Frances Croake Frank (quoted in *Vashti's Voices*, Autumn 2003):

Did the woman say
When she beheld him for the first time in the dark of a stable,
After the pain and the bleeding and the crying
'This is my body, this is my blood'?
Did the woman say
When she held him for the last time in the dark rain on a hilltop,
After the pain and the bleeding and the dying
'This is my body, this is my blood'?
Well that she said it to him then,
For dry old men,
Brocaded robes belying barrenness
Ordain that she not say it for him now.

It puzzled and frustrated me that Marists and the others got to imitate Mary by being priests, and preaching the Gospel, while women were meant to imitate her by being good little mothers and housewives! But I knew none of this was Mary's fault – it was people who were responsible for the contortions of her image. So she was rejected as a model for my real life, except as the First Disciple, and Woman of Faith. My primary energy had been given to my relationship with Jesus. I saw no need for her mediation. He was God Incarnate. She wasn't. End of story. And I just hated the sexist power-ridden metaphor that went 'God the Father is like the Chairman of the Board, Jesus is the Managing Director, the Holy Spirit is the Public Relations Officer, and Mother Mary sits at Reception.' My God was not distant and I had no need of a go-between!

But then in 2006 came my Goddess pilgrimage to Crete, led by thealogian Carol Christ. In the intervening years, my image of God had become more and more necessarily feminine. I am made in the image of God. I am a woman – so what did that say about the nature of the Divine One? With a God who was now 'She', and might even be called Goddess, Mary was even less relevant.

As related in the story of the pilgrimage, I was very shocked to realize bit by bit that Mary was being identified as Goddess. To a cradle Catholic this was verging on the blasphemous, made no sense at all. But I needed to understand how Carol and others I'd met at the San Francisco conferences got to that way of thinking.

I brought home my little Minoan goddess figure from 5000 years ago, bare breasted, elaborately dressed and holding aloft her two snakes of wisdom and power. And as I pondered the enormity of the questions 'Is Mary Goddess?' 'What is there here for me to learn?' I put her onto my Brigid's Cloak beside the cream Madonna, and said to them 'Talk to each other and let me know!' And with Rilke I learned to live the questions until some years later the answers have begun to arrive.

I had to start from the Catholic end of the conversation – the leap was too great otherwise. *The Mary Myth: On the Femininity of God* by Fr Andrew M. Greeley[23] did the trick. He explains how the great old myths of feminine deities attached themselves to the human Mary. And for a book published in 1977, there are some astonishing statements:

Catholic apologists have made a serious mistake by denying the obvious connection between Mary and the goddesses of pagan antiquity.

She (Mary) quite properly emerges as the Madonna, because she is the sacrament of Yahweh our loving mother.

Mary is the Catholic Christian religion's symbol which reveals to us that the Ultimate is androgenous…

Mary, the Christian mother goddess, is an obvious and natural symbol to reflect the femininity which is blended with masculinity in the androgenous God.

So I think I'm starting to get it! Mary as Goddess no longer seems outrageous. If Jesus is the human historical incarnation of the Holy One, so can she be too.

And I've figured there are differences in semantic understandings. For me, 'Goddess' means the Divine, the Ultimate, the one beyond the names. For those others it seems to mean any manifestation or image, historical or mythic, of the maternal and feminine archetype. For me 'worship' is the old catechism definition, the acknowledgement given to the Holy One alone. For others it seems to mean any honouring or veneration. Maybe we are not done yet, Mary and me.

Maybe there will be more to discover. Not quite sorted, but at least progress is being made in understanding her as symbol, as Goddess.

2010

Relationships

Relationships

Faith plays out in the context of our daily relationships with the Divine, with ourself, with others. In the days before computer screen wallpaper, I saw the 'I am here' words moving with creative energy through all that is, including my own being. Believing that at a gut level is still a work in progress! There have been special human relationships that have moved the process along, including those with my wonderful mother-in-law, and the psychotherapist I worked with over several years. They gave me opportunities to earth, to ground, to embody healthier human connectedness with myself and others.

And I learned the infinite complexity of the human person, the record of experiences that exists at our cellular level, beyond the reach of the intellect and conscious memory. I learned that acceptance of and compassion for the wounded disfigured parts of myself is so sacred, so healing. We are indeed wonderfully made! And with Irenaeus, I believe 'The glory of God is the human being fully alive.'

Friends have been crucially important. Holy Wisdom as Friend, rather than any of the old distance-creating words, makes so much sense, is so appealing. Sometimes this Presence is clearly perceptible in encounters and connections with others. Other times faith is needed! Grandchildren, in utero and beyond, are my delight, and work relationships in chaplaincy can be both joyful and challenging. And then, as there has always been, there is Jesus. When I was confused about which of the multiple 'To God' signposts to follow, he told me to hold his hand, close my eyes and he would take me the way that was right for me. I believe he has honoured that promise. He has come with me on all these explorations, the best of friends, companions and teachers. When, maybe twenty years ago, he dressed me in a rainbow sari and gave me a red tika, I didn't wonder why he was using Hindu symbolism. The journey goes on!

Presence

Where are you, God?
And then the words
Words within and words without –
I am here

A resonance that permeates, pervades
A whisper echoing through the universe
A song in the depths of my being –
I am here

Words of love, words of joy
Consoling words, creation words
Nowhere unspoken –
I am here

Burning bush that startles
Fine edged sword that knows
No boundaries of skin or heart –
I am here

Glimpse of simple sentence
Stretched through time
Reassurance of sustaining –
I am here

Effervescent words, ineluctable words
Indwelling, inebriating words
Silent words dancing words –
I am here

And I caught up in the dance
Am present to the All in all!

1992

Words
that move
through all
that is.

Words

Where are your words?
I weep, my friend
For your words
The tools and toys and treasures
Of your life
Words written
Words worked with
Words as pleasures and play
And now

They're not where you can catch them
Scattered like unruly sheep
Beyond the sheepdog mind now
To bring them into the pen of speech
One by one
In orderly array

Or worse they've disappeared
Like eels in underwater sludge
At the bottom of the barrel
As you grope muddily
For the one you need

Please don't work so hard
Maybe then the sheep
Will graze their way
Back across the field
Or as the water clears
You'll glimpse the one you need
And get an easier catch

As words weaken
And that way of connecting wanes
We'll have to walk a different way
Just holding hands

1997

My beloved mother-in-law Columba, poet, artist, teacher, encourager, and soul-mate had suffered a series of minor strokes.

For Columba

I walked early to the end of our road
Black early with golding gauze bubbles
Easing the clear and concrete path
Starbursts glimpsed in darker spaces

Then beyond the lights
Walking the unpathed place
Blind need for faith and courage
Thinking of you dying
And how I can only hold your hand
To the end of the road
You'll step out alone from there
Into the unknown land

Eyes adjusted to the dark
Glory of jewelled sky
Caught breath and soul
Dancing worlds inviting you
To flight in God
A long and wondering gaze

Then earthbound still
I turned back down
Tear-blurred towards the dawn
Tree shapes soon stole blackness
From the sky
Stars faded and blackbird
Launched song into silence

1997

And then the
major stroke
and imminent
death.

147

Saints Alive!

A miracle that made its way into a national newspaper and onto radio news.

My mother-in-law Columba loved the Saints – in particular Francis ('He got it right!'), Therese of Lisieux ('Sends a rose to answer questions'), Joseph ('Good at finding homes, did that for his Family') and of course, Anthony with his traditional ministry of finding lost stuff. They weren't really part of my package – I preferred unmediated prayer, and why not? But I've had to have another look…

This part of the story starts in February with my pilgrimage to Hiruharama with a group of spiritual directors. When I got home I realised I had Columba's copy of James K Baxter's *Jerusalem Day Book* on my shelf, unread. Read it, loved it deeply, talked about it, lent it to someone who expressed interest. Said it was precious, a short-term loan. Asked for its return a few weeks later. It couldn't be found! A few more weeks of searching – ditto. Desperate, and with my tongue somewhat in my cheek, I said that Columba would have prayed to St Anthony, and perhaps we could try that. Three days later it turned up, we rejoiced – and I did say 'thank you' to the heavenly helper.

A month down the track, I returned from a week away to a series of excited telephone messages from the rest-home where Columba had lived, and where she died in 1997. 'We've found that book!' Now 'that book' was no ordinary book, in fact it is unique! It is an album, hand-illuminated and gold high-lighted in Celtic style, made for Columba's father Carbra McGann to mark his retirement in 1923 from his position as Senior Science Inspector for all Ireland. Each of its dozen pages is a wonderful work of art, with ornate capitals and entwined patterns, some strangely reminiscent of Māori art. And it is signed by a bevy of bishops, superioresses(!) and rectors of all the schools he'd visited nationwide, as this was before the Partition of Ireland.

He was a remarkable man, born in 1861 as the eldest of nine, in a two-room cottage in Dunmanway, South Cork. He got his first pair of shoes aged 9 – a gift from the local nuns, who couldn't bear seeing his bleeding chilblains when he served their early morning masses. On leaving school at 12, he became an apprentice teacher, continued his education alongside his work, married at 47, and was by then sufficiently prosperous to take his much-younger bride to Switzerland for their honeymoon. I still have their souvenir goat-bell, and the amethyst rosary beads she was given by the bishop who married them. He also installed memorial windows to his parents Anne and Patrick McGann in the choir loft of the parish church in Dunmanway.

He was obviously much respected to have been given such a wonderful gift on his retirement, accompanied, it says, by some 'silver gift'. There is no artist's signature to be found, so I suspect it was a monk who was the scribe, someone wonderfully skilled in the traditional arts that go back to the Book of Kells and beyond.

This book had been lost before Columba died, despite efforts of the home staff to find it, and we grieved its loss. Another search after her death, including a newspaper article and visits to second-hand bookshops, was equally fruitless. It was gone. And more or less let go, though I wondered from time to time what had happened to it.

And now, startlingly, it is back! What a celebration as the story unfolded! Columba had lent it to a friend down the hall. They had both forgotten that, as old ladies can do. Her friend died aged 100 in 2001. Her relations boxed up the belongings and put them in their spare room. And only this month unpacked them, then realising the book was precious and 'not hers', contacted the home. Wonderfully, a staff member was still there who remembered the saga and search of over ten years previously. A few phone calls, a courier, and now it is home! Is it too fanciful to connect this return of another of Columba's missing books with my un-faithfilled words to St A? Was he proving a point? Did these two women get together and jog his celestial elbow? Not just one, but two missing books returned! Whatever – it's given me cause to ponder! I am grateful and overjoyed, astonished and humble. Perhaps I can make a little more room for him, for those other saints in my life. Perhaps they can be more acknowledged as members of my faith whanau. The kaleidoscope has turned once more!

2007

Eclipse

The conjunction of another approaching death, a new birth and signs in the heavens.

The day is bright outside, bright with promise
The baby squirms greyly on the screen
Her friend lies in the other ward, stunned at the news:
she is going to die
Her daughter lies on the couch, awe written serenely
On her face as she sees her half-gestated child
The cancer has spread to the liver – it is inoperable
The baby waves its arms and legs
Her friend has two months to live
Her grandchild will be born at Christmas
She holds out her arms to her friend and they cry together
Then baby's brain is scanned
A little walnut neatly divided in two
The CAT scan picked up the secondary tumours
Its 20 week old heart is pulsing strongly
Only love can help now
A story being conceived –
We saw you in your nest before you were born

The moon bites into the sun and the birds stop singing
Death bites into life and the light dims
Moment of darkness flared with fire and the world stands still
Joy bites into pain
She is far too young to die.
The baby unfurls its sea-anemone hands
Earth shakes with these happenings
It will never be the same again
Light and dark across each other's faces
They speak of what they'll do together in the time that's left
Looks like you're having a little girl!
And the birds begin
To sing again

1999

Dream Child

I was blessed to do long
term psychotherapy with
a gifted, generous woman.
It is not exaggerating to
say she saved my life.
Psychotherapy produces
dreams and poems!

Dream-child lost
Panic fear guilt
Stream of many pools
Rock-turned and churned
The deepest darkest
Of them all –
She must be there
First try fruitless
Again a driving
Painful
Dive
To the distant depth
Gather the bundle
That must be her
Strain to surface
It's been too long
She must be dead
How could I let this
Happen?
Unending grief
Now back on land
Up-ending sealed-faced child
And stranger doll
Mysterious flood
From puppet-mouth
How had that one
Taken on
The water-weight?

And when the pouring
Stopped
The child
Began to breathe again
To smile and be alive
She'd been sealed off
To just survive
The fear-created puppet-doll
Not needed now
Holding her tight
To reassure us both
A shallow pool
A place to play
And tadpoles
Future princesses
Tickled our hands
She laughed and played
We could put them in a jar
To watch legs grow
And tail dissolve
But let them go and grow
In their own way
Away from prying eyes
Two tiny arms warm
Curled around my neck
She's back where she belongs
And I am glad!

2001

Culmination

A major break-through moment.

Beyond the fear
The need
The forbidden deeply
Buried long hidden need
The Demon the Danger
Given time
Escaped the box
Shattered concrete
Leaped from churning gut
Disrupted diaphragm
Exploded into daylight
Puncturing pride eluding
Independence
Demanding
acknowledgement of
Its infant right to be

Need met by gentle arms
Hologrammed through
searing pain
Dark disbelief terrified hope
To potent peace
Re-ordered inner being
Connected severed soul
And changed the world
forever
Need transformed from
ravening demon

To sobbing child
And unless you become as a
little child
You shall not enter the realm
of The Divine
Marvel of paradox –
Abundance of what had been
Despairingly let go
The gift the blessing
The holding
The release the tears
The restoration
Of what was aeons since torn
away

Being reborn is a Christmas
miracle
A divine Girl-Child
Released from confinement
after
Jagged and gentle
Mythic pilgrim labour
Possible only with a midwife's
Integrity faithful tenacity
Generous patience
And honest gift of self
Long may we both dream
And dance the fullness
Of the world!

2002

And then…

Old fear,
new resolution.

Despite the joy
Or maybe its needful
Shadow a black and
Rock-toothed chasm
Opened at my feet
Of fear that you
You too
Would just forget
And leave me once again alone
With guilty shame
At having misread the signs

This time
A rope around my waist
A hand to hold a torch to shine
A map to read
I have not fallen in
The pledge that
You'll remember
That yes, this journey
Will be with us till we die
Dispels the fear and fear of shame
Joy tiptoes back

2003

White

There've been two sorts of white
One the bleak white-out
Of fear before the
Mountain hits
Couldn't think
Couldn't feel
Didn't understand
The questions
Let alone know the answers
And in the end
A new white place
Of grateful awe
Where marble glowed
And wondrous faces
Flowers fruits and ferns
Gleamed gently
To be finger-felt in full
Before the words arrived

2003

Separating

It's hard to know
Whether to pull
The petals
All off together
In one hard handful
And get it over with
Or wait gently
Till they let go
One by one
Of their own accord
Maybe this way
Improves the fruit

2003

Therapy had to come
to an end, though
it was some time
before this happened.
Altogether one of
the most blessed
experiences of my life.

The Cross

A gift from a man at my chaplaincy was a real challenge.

He gave me a cross
A cross to bear
It's huge
It's too heavy
It's ugly
Quite frankly it's gross
He gave me a cross to wear
Couldn't possibly
I'd rather be dead than
Seen with that around my neck
Tinny silver on a chunky chain
Ostentatious
Is an understatement
So very not me

And yet
It has this cloak of meaning
He gave me it from
The depths of his poverty
The depths of his illness
The depths of his love
The depths of his respect
This must be honoured
This makes it precious
He would be so happy
To see the gift appreciated
One day soon
I will wear that cross
I will bear that cross

Amen

2009

'I Call You Friends'

> My friends have been a hugely important part of my life, and still are!

Being sixty is worth a celebration. Still young enough to have a memory of the good times and the challenges. Old enough to be past the treadmill stuff, the years of having to run in order to stay in the same place. Young enough to be tolerably fit, and enjoy good health and the joys of getting out into the bush for some significant walking. Old enough to have seen a few friends die before we were ready. Young enough to know to celebrate those who are still here with extra affection – who knows what tomorrow will bring! I passionately want them all to be still around when I celebrate my 90th! Old enough to recognise that energy put into changing the world is better spent elsewhere when it becomes a matter of brick walls and headaches. Young enough (at last, again) to enjoy blowing bubbles, with or without a grandchild as an apprentice!

And so I've planned myself a birthday 'feast of friends'. They have mostly tended to be in separate boxes: the walking friends, the women's group friends, the friends from my 1980s prayer community, and so on. But at this party I want them all to meet each other! They are collectively the family I have made for myself to supplement my family of origin, and without their help and support, I simply wouldn't have made it this far!

There won't be time on that occasion to tell everyone why each one is so special. We would be there all night and all the next day too. Friends from school days, from university, from work and training courses, neighbours, and those who have shared the journey of faith. The sorts of memories I have are these: of the friend with whom I shared the learnings and satisfactions of becoming a solo parent and who is now launched on an academic career; of another who sent her husband up the road with their motor mower to do my lawns when my husband died; of the one who at 11.30pm on my first Christmas of solo parenting came to fix the suddenly-flat tyre of the six-year-old's Christmas bike; and of the family who for several years welcomed that same child into their home nearly every Sunday after church. It is true that it takes a whole village to bring up a child, let alone half a dozen!

There have been those who listened to me during the hard times – it must have been hard work, and sometimes apparently endless. Some could understand extra-well because they had had similar experiences themselves. Others with love were willing to try to understand. For that I will be ever grateful. Some have provided practical help, others loyalty beyond what I could have imagined. Others have been generously available on the phone. I have been truly blessed!

And no, I don't suppose the giving has been all one way. There has to be a reciprocity to keep things respectful. But by and large, learning to receive and accept kindness is a whole heap harder than giving! I was uncomfortable in our thirteen carless years because of all the necessary lifts given by kind and helpful souls – for shopping, to doctors, to school functions. Very uncomfortable! Until the day a friend pointed out that this situation was an opportunity for them to show love. If there were no willing receivers, she said, there could be no givers! I was in fact doing them a favour by accepting what was offered! And while I was not in a position to repay her for those kindnesses, she expressed confidence that when I could, I would pass it on to someone else.

Hmm!! That was a conversion experience of sorts: I did indeed have to pray for the grace to let them serve me, to receive gracefully. The image occurred to me of these loving kindnesses as the blood circulation in the Body of Christ. It's what keeps the Body alive and vibrant as it moves around from cell to cell to cell. Times have changed, and it still gives me pleasure to do the passing on, and give people rides in the car that I eventually acquired. With the help of this community of friends my children have grown into decent adults, and have families of their own. I can wish them nothing better than good friends to accompany them through their adult years.

Friendship – this is what Jesus offers us (John 15,15). From my friends I have learned more of what to expect of my relationship with him: love, generosity, consistency, preparedness to accept the validity of my perspective, to understand, to support whether in practical or other ways. It is what I try to offer in return - to him and to them. 'Whatsoever you do' to another, you 'do unto him'. We have been blessed by my friends, he and I both!

2002

A God-friend

A youngish man, early thirties, came to our charismatic prayer group, woebegone, grieving for a marriage that he wanted to restore. We welcomed him, nurtured him, worked with him on our corporate ministry of praise and worship. And rejoiced as he healed, matured and became in his turn someone who could minister to others.

> Many people have the experience of thinking of someone close then having them make contact. Some call it Divine Choreography!

Some time down the track, he told more of his story: a suicide attempt, only thwarted by a friend with a 'funny feeling' who went round, saw the car, couldn't raise anyone and called the police. Time in the psychiatric ward. A profound experience of God in a motel and an approach to a church. A priest who heard his confession and gave him his first Eucharist in years. A return to Catholic origins. A retreat where he observed some joyful people and wanted what they had. And so to the prayer group. And then as more detail emerged, the penny dropped!

Our somewhat sceptical parish priest had come to us a couple of years earlier with a request that sounded more like a challenge. He was counselling a married couple, both 'hopeless cases' and he 'couldn't do a thing with them'. So please would we pray for them. 'And', he said, 'if the Holy Spirit pulls this one off, I'll eat my hat!' This was a serious promise – he was a Capuchin with a long brown serge pointy hood! So each of them had someone praying specifically for them every day for an extended period. Sadly the marriage had not been resurrected, but here was the husband who had found his way to the very people who had been praying for him!

The suicide attempt would, without interruption, have been effective. When he was assessed at the hospital, staff said he would have lived only another half hour without treatment. Our oldest son became his shop delivery person as an after school job. And so began a long tradition of my teenagers delivering prescriptions for the pharmacy under that owner and the next. All except the youngest, as, sadly, by then the shop was closed.

We came to appreciate B deeply as he became a very caring and communicating person, supportive of the other group members and with a particular passion for the ministry of visiting prison. Then he went off to Bible College to develop his gifts and skills and seek a life direction. He came back knowing that he was going to head to Australia to be part of a charismatic community based there. But it would take a little while.

My husband suggested that he should come and board with us. I was delighted with the idea, not least because I saw him as a wonderful role model for our teenage sons. He was kind, considerate and generous, and we became very close. My husband at this stage was drinking heavily which virtually eliminated any possibility of reasonable communication. He also travelled a lot for work, so was often absent for any family crises. We hadn't owned a car for several years, which meant a degree of difficulty managing shopping, doctors and so on. B put his car at my disposal a couple of times a week which was a huge gift. And when one of my little ones took the end off his thumb, I rang him at work, he dropped everything and came and ran us to doctor and hospital. It meant a lot!

It was a totally honourable friendship – we were both completely true to our respective marriage vows. Our commitment to live with God as our first priority kept us focussed on respect for each other and each other's commitments. He was an amazing support to me during my last pregnancy which could have ended up fatally for both mother and child. Both with prayer and practical assistance. He brought husband over to the hospital when the baby finally arrived safely! It was right that he should be the godfather.

And then the time came for him to go to Australia. First he had to sell his business, then decide what to do with the proceeds. He had committed to giving away a major part of his possessions and starting a new life in a covenant community. I'd never seen anyone do this before! He asked whether I had any ideas about deploying the funds. Strangely, just the previous week some bridging finance on our house had been called up, $30,000 to be precise. This had been let run over way past the agreed limit since we bought the place six years earlier. I had no idea how it could be refinanced and was pretty worried. B thought and prayed about it for a couple of days and then came back with a startling proposal. He would give us $30,000, and we in turn would make quarterly payments to four charities that he nominated until it all had been given away a second time. And yes, we should pay interest, at a then very generously low 10%. We agreed with enormous relief and gratitude.

This was 1980 when interest rates were going through the roof. Husband and I met a work colleague of his in town who had just been to refinance his own mortgage – at 23%. He asked what we were paying. We told him 10%. 'Jesus!' he exclaimed. 'Yes!' we agreed. But didn't explain how accurate his comment was!

And so B went to Brisbane and embraced his new life with dedication and enthusiasm. Some sporadic communication continued, the very occasional phone call. I missed him a lot.

In 1984 I woke in the middle of one night and heard a Voice telling me 'I fed you on manna and quail in the desert of your life. I am honouring you because you took no more than your portion, and your children will be blessed in turn'. I knew that this was about my relationship with B, and was awed by the scripture reference. Life had indeed been a desert. It still was! I was not too surprised to hear from B a few days later that he had become engaged to J. I wished them well. And was a bit startled at the intensity of my own reaction. It was one thing knowing he was 'not mine', but totally different knowing he was now 'someone else's'.

A few days later again, I took the children to a Sunday afternoon mass as husband had been on a weekend retreat. My knees gave way with shock as the priest began with the prayer 'Lord, you have fed us on manna and quail in deserts of our lives'. And I realised how beautifully I had been sustained through this transition time by the same Words that came before and after like a double anchor.

They got married. My husband died in 1986. A couple of years later life was still pretty turbulent, but differently. My daily prayer time was a necessity. I was working my way through the Sadhana book of meditations. I sat on my porch in the sun. The task of the day was to remember a happy period of one's life, and re-live it with gratitude. I had wrapped that precious time when B was with us and put it away in a memory drawer. Here was an invitation to bring it out and relive it. It didn't seem a great idea, but I decided to accept.

And so I reminisced about the good times, the joys of having someone in my life and in the house who actually wanted to understand and support. I thanked our God for the blessings of these times, and prayed that the new marriage would be fulfilling for them both. It was a good experience. After the prayer time, I closed the book and stood up. Before I'd taken a step the phone rang. It was B ringing from Australia saying 'The Holy Spirit told me to ring you up'. Once again I was dumfounded!

Many years have passed since then. Twice I have visited and found the same easy loving companionship with them both. Our theologies have diverged. Any permanent relationship between us could well have foundered on such things. The trust and the respect continue. A very special friendship that was indeed manna and quail in the desert of my life continues still, even now that I live in peaceful meadows.

2010

Postscript: I emailed the draft of this story to B for his comment, and got a startled reply. He had just the previous day decided to ring me, to see what I remembered of his time with us, as he'd felt a prompting to write his own faith story. We both acknowledged with awe that the God-connection continues!

God as 'Friend'

More on friendship – this time as an image of the Holy One.

For a change, the 6pm news that night warmed many hearts. As reporters fired questions at him, David Bain's refrain was 'My friends, my friends!' 'How have you survived the last 13 years?' 'My friends, my friends!' 'How are you going to celebrate?' 'My friends, my friends! I just want to be with my friends.' To them he attributed his sanity and courage. And the consistent loyalty and support he has received have given many cause to ponder on both the awesome significance and the cost of friendship.

A dictionary definition gives 'friend: a person known well to another and regarded with liking, affection and loyalty; an intimate' and 'an ally in a fight, a cause; a supporter'. A friend is someone who understands how things are for you, who will sit beside you, who is 'on your team'. Is this how we are with our friends? Is this what we receive from others? There's the old saying 'If you want to have a friend, be one.' And yes, friendship can be literally and truly salvific, that is, healing and life-giving. It matters so much!

Robert Wicks on his recent speaking tour of Aotearoa New Zealand spoke of the huge importance of friendships in sustaining a healthy lifestyle, particularly for those in a caring/ ministry role to others. We should ideally have, he said, at least one of each of four sorts of friends. There are the prophetic ones who challenge us, the 'sloppy sentimental' ones who will always take our side, and defend us against whatever may threaten, the ones with humour who will tease, lighten us up, and the spiritual ones who call us to be all we can be without embarrassing us about where we are.

It seems in recent years that men are learning more of what women have known forever – 'being real' with friends, one or more, is a way to relieve stress and share joys as well as sorrows. Describing recent research from UCLA , Gale Berkowitz says it has been discovered that women experiencing stress are hormonally programmed to another option beyond the 'fight or flight' response. This has been labelled 'befriending'.

'In fact,' one of the researchers says:

> 'it seems that when the hormone oxytocin is released as part of the stress responses in a woman, it buffers the 'fight or flight' response and encourages her to tend children and gather with other women instead. When she actually engages in tending or befriending, studies suggest that more oxytocin is released, which further counters stress and produces a calming effect'.

And in times of danger female elephants gather the calves and form a circle round them.

Many other studies have found that social ties reduce our risk of disease by lowering blood pressure, heart-rate, and cholesterol. The results of this recent research were so significant, that it was concluded that 'not having close friends or confidantes is as detrimental to your health as smoking or carrying extra weight'!

Jesus told the disciples he now called them his friends rather than servants (John15:14-15). He wanted them to know that he regarded them with affection and loyalty, as his intimates. And because friendship is not a one way street, the corollary was that they could and should regard him as their friend too, rather than as Lord and Master. In our own lives, who gives us more comfort and inducement to grow – a powerful person to whom we feel subservient, or a friend?

And Jesus as the image of the Divine points to the friendship of God for each one of us. How much more appealing is a God who has compassion and understanding for us, whom we can trust to help us achieve our best selves! God as Best Friend! God who never uses the deadly playground weapon of seven-year-olds: 'I'm not going to be your friend any more!' It is tragic to come across people still who are afraid of God, terrified of 'His' condemnations and judgements. It is no coincidence that often that was the experience they had of their own fathers who were not in any sense experienced as 'friends'.

Many have rejected 'a God like that', and understandably so. If only the friendship of God was consistently taught as the fundamental invitation to us! It was a huge shift in my own journey when I was drawn to start wondering what God, my Friend, wanted **for** me rather than **from** me! The answer: abundant life. The question: what changes need I make to my world-view and actions to receive this generous gift? Our wounds can limit what we expect and therefore what we are able to receive.

Then there is the invitation to be our own best friends, in the sense of taking responsibility for our own growth and well-being. Am I being a better friend to myself when I indulge the 'need' to enjoy a large block of chocolate or when I choose not to? More seriously, as a counsellor, I often find a significant task for clients is to learn the same degree of compassionate understanding for themselves as they would for a friend. To release their self-condemnations and judgements, and to be kind to themselves instead. For healing, the verse 'Love your neighbour as yourself' often needs to be re-versed: 'Love yourself the way you love your neighbour'.

So with God as our Friend, we are offered the assurance of Someone who is 'for' and 'with' us, who will inspire and invite us to grow, will make us laugh on occasion, will relieve our stress by hearing our difficulties, enhance our well-being, and encourage us to befriend ourselves and others. A God who believes in each of us, in the best of who we are, and in our power to offer this sort of friendship to others. Expect, and you will not be disappointed!

2007

Remember the Rainbow?

Do you remember
The day they said
Go to a special place
And meet Jesus there?

So I went where water fell
Cliff length to a bubbling pool
Stones for steps across the shallows
Sun and sparkle and in the spray
A rainbow

And waited
Standing on a rock
Expectant

You came smiling
Hopping across the rocks
Pleased to be there
With me
And on the way along
Gathered the rainbow
Over your arm

Then as I watched entranced
You draped it round me as sari
Beautiful shimmering silk
All the colours
And I was transformed

Then with total tenderness
From somewhere you produced
The red dot for my forehead
I did not know then
What that meant

2009

> Jesus was at the beginning of the journey, and is here still as Way of life, Truth of life, Life of life.

And now...

And Now...

It is time to bring the many and varied ponderings to some coherent conclusion. The assembling and finishing of a quilt is itself a significant task. The top with its patterns and colours is the most visible component. There are also the batting, the inner warmth that becomes hidden, and the backing. These last two pieces equate to those elements.

Then the binding.

As the 'batting', my personal inside world has gradually become simpler, more intentionally attuned to the Ultimate Cosmic Reality, Cosmic Christ-Sophia. Silence, simplicity and solitude offer a way through for the human race. They are the conditions for the inner journeys that are so crucial to our well-being, and the abundant life that we have been promised. And this happens in the ordinariness of everyday life. When I and several of my walking friends turned 65 in 2007 we had a P party to celebrate becoming pensioners. We dressed up as poets, peasants and other obvious P-words, and dined on pate, pretzels, pumpkin, pasta, pork, pavlova and pinot noir. A lot of fun! This transition prompted my pondering on the pleasures of Life Now. And that is how life still is a few years later!

In the external 'backing'/background beyond my home, one dimension of the world becomes ever more complex in terms of technology, power and politics. But there is also a core dimension of humanity where so many Truth-seekers, be they scientists, thealogians and theologians, spiritual journeyers, poets and others are discovering how much they have in common. The paths converge!

Then the 'binding' for the whole quilt: I have discovered over the years that entrusting oneself ever more completely to Divine Love is a fundamental process on the spiritual journey. Then the adventure of discovering oneself, and oneself in relationship with All that Is becomes possible. These explorations of mine have been an affirmation of that Presence.

My Goddess – or Life – or the Universe – opens up new ways of being for all of us, leading the willing to the emptiness that is the fullness. All is One!

Life @65

My garden mostly minds
Its own business
So I am astonished and grateful
When flowers bloom
Lettuces grow among the roses
Rhubarb gives a feed or two
And the lily buds
From goodness knows where
Are ready to open any minute
Will they be scented?
And will they come again?

I love my bedroom
Our original oak bedroom suite
Forty-five years old this year
Dark exposed beams with
Little shelves for special things
Like the silver powder compact
Brought for my mother
From Bethlehem during the War
Souvenirs of Chartres
Heidelberg and Grassmere
Wine-red velvet curtains
Here when I came
Velvet cushion made to match
On which sits Edwina bear
The other two walls
White with old-fashioned tracery
Of flowers
The bed my safe warm sanctuary
Crisp white broderie anglaise
Electric blanket deserves a hymn
Of praise all to itself
A vital accessory to living alone
Nothing like getting into
A warm bed on a cold night

A good way to sum up, a
quilt of the everyday sacred,
still as true as when written.

Around my house
Creative women's works
Twelve year-old Silva Vallentine
Finished her minute stitching
Of sepia mill and wheel in 1846
Laura's gorgeous collage and embroideries
Vivienne's 3D painting of purple blue
And brown Aotearoa hills

My cross-stitched unicorns
Then I too learned to paint
And while still finding my way
Burning Bush Dancing Star
Fall Leaves and Waterfall
Are surprisingly better than just ok

Gratitude to and for a body that
That has served me well
Flourishes pain-free still
And bore my children
With care it will last
A while longer
In this place of sacred pleasures
Sight taste hearing smell and touch

The joy of waking to bird-song
The music of the aeons
Cicadas striating the sunshine
Ferry drawing a line
Across harbour mill-pond
Roadside pohutukawas red
Windows and pores all open to
Receive summer
Warm grass under bare feet
As washing gets hung out
It'll be dry in an hour
Then worship at the shrine
Of the latest perfect rosebud

My children are adults now
Sources of pride
And sometimes pain
I'd like them to know me
As another human being
Who has simply done her best
Wonderful to be at this fulcrum
Remembering two generations
Back seeing two forwards
Tracking genes
And variations thereof
Hope for the future
In an uncertain world
For each exquisite grand-child
Hope their parents' strengths
Will tend these little lives
As each one needs

Friends are jewels
Those of half a century
And those met last week
The every-week ones
And the Christmas only ones
Shared commitments to justice
For women
Understanding
Love of life and each other
Loyalty and hope

A good walk up Kaukau
Going from here spreads the climb
Scrutinised by nosey cattle
Sunbaked views of J-ville Porirua
And the Sounds
Once a tiny ferry sidled
Into the hills beyond Cook Strait
And disappeared
Coming down through bush
A breeze
Steps happily made for shorter legs
Children playing in stream and park
A well-deserved latte
Before trekking home

Windless days an aberration
'Look the leaves are still'
Loving a warm north breeze
Strong enough to dance my hair
And cool the effort of climbing
Then the southerly shriekers
Over 100kph

Creaks and shakes mean
I sleep downstairs those nights
Walking round the block in gale
Can exhilarate
Hanging onto lamp-post
At the crest of the hill
Laughing out loud
Waiting for storm to draw breath
So I can start the downward plunge

In Wilton Bush
Red of nectared flax flowers
And newly unfurled ferns
Purple of poroporo and rangiora veins
Brown of stream plinking and swishing
Through mossy rocks
White of kereru whirr
Grey of aging bark skins
Blue of back-drop branch spaces
Green of soft moss
and exuberant leaves
Gold of leaf-fall and tūīs' gargling

Twice weekly swims start days off well
After cider vinegar and honey
In warm water
Thirty plus lengths
Thinking about Life
And those I love
Enjoying turtle-shell patterns
Of light on underwater tiles
Breathing out completely
Both body and soul
Makes good space for breathing in
The rituals of drying dressing
And chats round off the pleasure

Patchwork is about seeking
Coherent whole a new pattern
Where all the fragments
Find a place
The purple daisies
With hand-quilted butterflies
On the downstairs bed
Was my first effort
Four Elements crazy quilt
Such fun – the bits and bobs
Saved for years all found a place
Lush and glittering it hung a while
Behind the altar at St Andrew's

Living alone is indeed
A glorious freedom
Though somewhat time-consuming
When one gardens cleans the car
Pays the bills buys the gifts
Spring cleans sorts the papers
That breed overnight
On the kitchen bench
Two last time I looked
Now seventeen
But there is no hurry
It all comes together
If dishes are not washed every day
And a pot of stew does three meals
No-one complains

Telephone a wondrous
Connector better than emails
Or texts
Still get a buzz when reaching
For the phone to ring a friend
And it rings and it's that one
Just beating me to it
Knowing it was time to talk

Little green car Estralita
Independence joy sine qua non
Of involvement with the world
Simple sturdy sure-footed
When I dream of a car
I know the story is about my life

Computer a companion
In the dance of words and thoughts
Typewriters carbon paper
Gestetners and pink correcting fluid
Remembered without nostalgia

And work – the precious privileged
Times on holy ground with those
Who want less pain
Or growth in God or just someone to say
How is it?
And hear the doings of the day
They do the work I am the listener

Simplicity the aim
No jewellery, make-up or tobacco
Occasional glass of wine
(Red, please)
Simple food
In solidarity with myriad women
With none to give their children
Mine never went hungry
But life was very basic
How many sausages could we get for
$1.87?
Could do marmite, but not jam
But we got by
Then a need now a choice

Sunny evening
Sitting outside hearing
Late bees visit honeysuckle
Enjoying coffee
And this morning's sudoku

My Goddess is in above
Around through beyond below
She dances with me
The dream the task the play
The creation the joy the pain
The work the rest the awe
Breathing singing always
I am here

With all of this
When the researcher asked
(At dinner time as always)
On a scale of one to ten
Where one is low and ten high
How do you rate your satisfaction
With your life?
I heard myself say Ten!
Thanks be to Her and all who love me!

2007

Converging Paths

This is what I see: many paths are converging. Those who journey with energy, integrity and persistence are recognizing common experiences, and that our differing languages, symbol systems and myths have a common Source and a common Home.

> As awareness grows of inter-spirituality, which is at a deeper level than interfaith, a new area for reflection opens up.

For many, women particularly, the paths of Christianity and Paganism are converging as Christian women claim the right to name the Holy One as they must – like themselves. They need to identify with the Goddess in themselves, and in the material world. And this is so compatible with an ongoing, indeed an enriched relationship with Jesus. I read recently the story of a Christian Witch – a combination many would call impossible. Without laying claim to her self-description, I recognized in her Pagan practice many of the same elements that have featured in Christian celebrations I've been part of: recognising the seasons, celebrating births and deaths in their many forms, honouring our aging and the trinity of virgin, mother, crone, Goddess as immanent, as permeating and healing the cosmos, the land and all that lives including ourselves. In our context these were Christian celebrations.

Adherents of the major traditions, at least in their mystical strands, are discovering common ground and understandings. Oneness with all that is. And such treasures there are to share. I love the Hindu net of Indra, all-that-is as an infinite net, with a jewel at each joining that reflects the entirety of everything everywhere else. A potent image for inter-connectedness. And in the west from science there is the concept of the cosmos as a hologram: any fragment contains the entirety of everything.

Science and religion are converging. I never could understand the reputed conflict between these two fields: science is about truth-seeking, God is another name for Truth. Where is the conflict? Granted, egos and vested interests have successfully fouled things in both fields in the past, but at their heart science and religion are two aspects of the same Search. Quantum physics and theology are converging. Prayer, possibilities and particles are being pondered in enlightening ways. Neurology and Evolutionary Science are studying the inner and communal experiences of prayer and faith-life. Brain science is revealing that intense focus shifts energy and makes an outcome likelier. That visualisations by sports people improve their performances is common knowledge. No longer do many of us image/imagine a somewhere-else God who opens random begging letters and randomly responds. Prayer changes us, rather than the mind of a remote and all-powerful God, to open us to both receiving and creating what we desire.

Old knowledge and new are converging. There is a growing respect in many First World people for the various age-old wisdoms of indigenous people. They have been able to set aside their rationalist colonizing consumer-driven cultures and to listen with respect to what First Peoples are telling us about ways to preserve, to save the planet. 'The earth is held in existence by the spiritual attention of the people' said the old aboriginal man out beyond Uluru. Western science and religion are becoming humbler and more willing to learn the old truths – or discovering that their 'new' knowledge has been there all along, albeit in a differently told story.

There is power in each of us to be recognized, owned and used in creative service. Jesus promised that we would do even greater things than he could do, and that his Spirit would lead us into all truth (John 14:12 and 16:17). This is a human reality that is recognized in the Pagan, Shamanic and other traditions. It has been largely suppressed and lost sight of in the Christian tradition. It is our birth-right, and those for whom this is already manifesting need not feel that they have to abandon their Christianity. Jesus-Sophia is there. In a potent DVD series, cosmologist Brian Swimme talks of how the powers that formed and enliven the cosmos are alive and accessible in each of us. And how, the more we are attuned to the Power of love, service and creativity, the more this will flow through us. Another way of describing the Holy Spirit?

Two people from a Catholic background, one still committed to parish life, met at a Buddhist workshop on Sky-dancing Dakini goddesses, and marvelled that a good half of the participants that day likewise had roots in Catholicism. They pondered the similarities between dakinis and angels. Dakinis wear a lot less, don't have wings and aren't blond, but are nevertheless archetypal guides, messengers, consolers and liberators. The idea of an inter-spirituality retreat was born, where people from different traditions could share practice and recognize common ground. So as this book goes to print, three people from each of seven traditions will be gathering for a weekend of shared meditation focussed on Compassion. This is the common heart of all seven. We will be from Shamanic, Hindu, Daoist, Buddhist, Jewish, Christian and Sufi traditions. Inter-spirituality is at a deeper level again than interfaith. It is more deeply about trust in the sharing of the treasures of the practice. It is about creating an energy field of compassion to help heal the planet and its people.

We are here to learn to love – the Holy, ourselves and others. Love is paying attention. Love is power. Love effects changes that we have called miracles.

So I claim my power now, knowing this is truly Divine, knowing Goddess/God is even more mysterious, more transcendent and more present than our older stories seemed to tell.

She is me!
She is you!
All is One!

2011

Endnotes

1. Waitangi Day (6 February) celebrates the 1840 Treaty between Māori and the British Crown and remembers its founding by Pakeha.
2. Anzac Day (25 April) a remembrance of Gallipoli 1915 and all the war deaths and service since.
3. 1989, p 181.
4. See p 75.
5. Parnell introduced the eight hour working day in NZ (1840).
6. Davies (1923-2005) was a leading trade unionist and feminist.
7. A final Kiwi Spirituality celebration was held in July 2010.
8. Based on a poem by Harold Thurman.
9. Community Learning Aotearoa New Zealand
10. First published in *Vashti's Voices*, No 2/8 Autumn 2001
11. Paterson G, in *Bread of Tomorrow*, ed Morley, J, SPCK & Christian Aid, London 1992
12. This Cosmic Walk workshop is available for use by other groups around New Zealand. Contact Sister Marcellin Wilson: marcellinsrm@xtra.co.nz
13. Cheyne C, *Made in God's Image. A Project Researching Sexism in the Catholic Church in Aotearoa New Zealand*. NZCBC, Wellington, 1990
14. Pearce M, *Sub-Ordination, A Study of Catholic Women's Preparedness for Ordination to Priestly Ministry*. Wellington, 1994
15. Quoted in *Vashti's Voices*, Autumn 2003
16. Sally Kennedy, *Faith and Feminism: Catholic Women's Struggles for Self-expression*, Studies in the Christian Movement, Sydney, 1985
17. Pat Matheson died in February 2010.
18. Sr P Rath, *A Guide to the Abbey of St Hildegard*, Trans B Thompson, Michael Imhof Verlag, Petersberg, 2003
19. Christ C., *Diving Deep & Surfacing*. 3rd ed. Beacon, Boston 1995, p 1
20. Bourgeault C, *The Wisdom Jesus, Transforming Heart and Mind – A New Perspective on Christ and His Message*. Shambala, Boston, 2008
21. Houston J, *The Search for the Beloved*. Penguin, US 1997
22. Concept based on DF McKee, *Two Can Toucan*. Andersen, London 1985
23. Bishop Geoffrey Robinson, Melbourne, 1998
24. Gimbutas MA, *The Language of the Goddess*. Harper SF, 1995
25. www.herchurch.org
26. www.reclaiming.org
27. www.sweethoney.com/lyrics
28. McBride T, *Faith Evolving: A Patchwork Journey*. (2005), p 95
29. Miles S, *Take This Bread*, Ballantine Books, NY, 2007
30. Chatwin B, *The Songlines*, Penguin, NY, 1987
31. James K. Baxter, Mother Aubert
32. Based on information sheets, Department of Conservation *Dominion Post*, 14 December 2007, Matiu Really Matters, November 2007
33. Check East by West website for current timetable and places served: https://eastbywest.co.nz/
34. McNeish J, *The Man from Nowhere and other prose*, Godwit Press, Auckland 1991
35. Personal communication
36. JM Tjibaou, *Cibau Cibau Kamo pa Kavaac*, Trans R Benyon (2000) Agence de developpement de la culture Kanak, Noumea, 1998
37. Fowler JW, *Stages of Faith: the Psychology of Human Development and the Quest for Meaning* (San Francisco: Harper, 1995, first published 1981).
38. Waldron, VR & Kelley DL, *Communicating Forgiveness*. Los Angeles: Sage Publications, 2008, 129.
39. Ibid, 132.
40. The Kairos Theologians, *The Kairos Document, Challenge to the Church* (Grand Rapids, Michigan: Wm. B. Eerdmans Publishing Co, 1986), 37-47.

[41] Taylor A JW, *Justice as a Basic Human Need*, New Ideas in Psychology, 21,3 (Nov 2003): 209-219.

[42] Hermans JL, *Trauma and Recovery.* London, Pandora, 1992, 189-90.

[43] The ! in !Kung represents a clicking sound in their language

[44] Richard Katz, *Kung Hunter-Gatherers, & The Kung Approach to Healing, Boiling Energy: Community Healing among the Kalahari Kung*, Cambridge, Harvard University Press, 1994, pp 30-56.

[45] Brain Story, Volume 1, BBC

[46] Griffiths B, *The Cosmic Revelation: The Hindu Way to God*, Templegate, London, 1994.

[47] Broomfield J, *Other Ways of Knowing: Recharting Our Future With Ageless Wisdom*, Inner Traditions, Rochester, Vermont, 1997

[48] The Catechism of the Catholic Church, Vatican 1992, para 2353

[49] Bullough VL, *Science in the Bedroom, a History of Sex Research*, Basic Books, NY 1994

[50] Bass E & Davis L, *Courage to Heal*, 1988

[51] First published in *The God Book: Talking about God Today*, ed. Neil Darragh, Accent Publications, Auckland NZ, 2008. pp 219-229

[52] Aquinas, *Summa Theologiae*, Article 9

[53] Paul Tillich, 1962

[54] Personal communication. This was Jim Cotter's original wording of his version of the Lord's Prayer, modified to 'Earth-maker, Pain-bearer, Life-giver' for inclusion in *A New Zealand Prayer-book, The Church of the Province of New Zealand*, Collins, 1989 (Anglican Prayer Book, p181)

[55] Mary Daly, *Beyond God the Father: Towards a Philosophy of Women's Liberation.* Beacon Press, Boston. 1973, pp 33, 34.

[56] Elizabeth A. Johnson, *She Who Is*, Crossroad, NY, 1992. pp 170-87

[57] Hot Winter Broth, Glynn Cardy, *Tui Motu InterIslands*, August 2007 p 20

[58] Marcella Althaus Reid, Geering Lectures, St Andrew's Trust, 2005

[59] Philip Culbertson & Tavita Maliko, *A g-string is not Samoan: Exploring a Trans-gressive Third-Gender Pasifika Theology. Concilium 324*, February 2008, pp. 62-72.

[60] Brian Swimme, *The Hidden Heart of the Cosmos*, Orbis, NY. 1996 Ch. 13, pp 97-104

[61] Elizabeth Johnson, op cit, p 119

[62] Edwina Gateley, *Warm Moist Salty God.* Source Books, 1993

[63] Mary Betz, *Who do I mean by God*, Tui Motu InterIslands, March 2005

[64] Congregation for the Doctrine of the Faith, Rome, 1 February 2008, www.vatican.va/roman_cuuria/congregations/cfaith/documents/rc_con_cfaith_do... for the Doctrine of the Faith, Rome, 1 February 2008, Accessed 28.8.08

[65] Kathryn Rountree, *Embracing the Witch and the Goddess*, Routledge, London 2004, p 133

[66] Carol Christ, *She Who Changes*, Palgrave Macmillan, New York, 2003, pp 92, 167-8

[67] The voice of women, the voice of God cf vox populi vox Dei

[68] www.herchurch.org

[69] Jann Aldredge-Clanton & Larry E Schultz, *Inclusive Hymns for Liberating Christians*, Eakin Press, Austin, 2006. no's 35 & 92

[70] Jann Aldredge Clanton, *In Whose Image? God and Gender*, Crossroad, NY. 2001

[71] Jann Aldredge Clanton, *In Search of the Christ Sophia*, 23rd Publications, Austin. 1995, 2nd ed 2004

[72] Traditional, based on 13th century hymn

[73] Andrew Greeley, *The Mary Myth: On the Femininity of God.* The Seabury Press, NY, 1977

Bibliography

Aldredge-Clanton J & Schultz LE, *Inclusive Hymns for Liberating Christians*. Eakin Press, Austin, 2006

Aldredge Clanton J, *In Whose Image? God and Gender*. Crossroad, NY. 2001 *In Search of the Christ Sophia*. 23rd Publications, Austin, 1995, 2nd ed 2004

Bass E & Davis L, *Courage to Heal*. 1988

Bourgeault C, *The Wisdom Jesus: Transforming Heart and Mind, A New Perspective on Christ and His Message*. Shambhala, Boston 2008

Broomfield J, *Other Ways of Knowing: Recharting Our Future With Ageless Wisdom, Inner Traditions*. Rochester, Vermont, 1997

Bullough, VL, *Science in the Bedroom, a History of Sex Research*, Basic Books, NY 1994

Chatwin B, *The Songlines*, Penguin, NY, 1987

The Catechism of the Catholic Church. Vatican 1992

Cheyne C, *Made in God's Image. A Project Researching Sexism in the Catholic Church in Aotearoa New Zealand*. NZCBC, Wellington, 1990

Christ C, *She Who Changes*. Palgrave Macmillan, New York, 2003

Diving Deep & Surfacing. 3rd ed. Beacon, Boston 1995

Daly M, *Beyond God the Father: Towards a Philosophy of Women's Liberation*. Beacon Press, Boston. 1973

Fowler JW, *Stages of Faith: the Psychology of Human Development and the Quest for Meaning*. San Francisco: Harper, 1995, first published 1981

Gateley E, *Warm Moist Salty God*. Source Books, 1993

Gimbutas MA, *The Language of the Goddess*. Harper, SF, 1995

Goulter MC, *Sons of France, a forgotten influence on New Zealand history*. Whitcombe and Tombs Ltd, Wellington, 1958

Greeley A, *The Mary Myth: On the Femininity of God*. The Seabury Press, NY, 1977

Griffiths B, *The Cosmic Revelation: The Hindu Way to God*. Templegate, London,1994

Hermans JL, *Trauma and Recovery*. Pandora, London, 1992

Houston J, *The Search for the Beloved*. Penguin, US 1997

Johnson EA, *She Who Is*. Crossroad, NY, 1992

The Kairos Theologians, The Kairos Document, Challenge to the Church. Grand Rapids, Michigan: Wm. B. Eerdmans Publishing Co, 1986

Katz R, *Kung Hunter-Gatherers, & The Kung Approach to Healing, Boiling Energy: Community Healing among the Kalahari Kung*. Cambridge, Harvard University Press, 1994

Kennedy S, *Faith and Feminism: Catholic Women's Struggles for Self-expression, Studies in the Christian Movement.* Sydney, 1985

Malacki Z, *Venerable Jerzy Popieluszko*, trans AJ Golabek, Wydawnicto Siostr Loretanek. Warsaw, 2002

McBride T, *Faith Evolving: A Patchwork Journey.* P McBride, Wellington 2005, 2nd ed 2007

McKee DF, *Two Can Toucan.* Red Fox, 1986

McNeish J, *The Man from Nowhere and other prose*, Godwit Press, Auckland 1991

Miles S, *Take This Bread.* Ballantine Books, NY, 2007

Pearce M, *Sub-Ordination, A Study of Catholic Women's Preparedness for Ordination to Priestly Ministry.* Wellington, 1994

Rath P, *A Guide to the Abbey of St Hildegard.* Trans B Thompson, Michael Imhof Verlag, Petersberg, 2003

Rountree K, *Embracing the Witch and the Goddess.* Routledge, London 2004

Slee N, *Women's Faith Development, Patterns and Processes.* Ashgate, Aldershot, 2004

St Clair A, *The Path of a Christian Witch.* Llewelyn, Woodbury Minn, 2010

Swimme B, *The Hidden Heart of the Cosmos.* Orbis, NY. 1996 *The Powers of the Universe.* DVD

Taylor AJW, *Justice as a Basic Human Need.* New Ideas in Psychology, 21, 3 Nov 2003

Tjibaou JM, Jean-Marie Tjibaou, *Cibaou Cibaou, Kamo pa Kavaac, Agence de développement de la culture Kanak.* 1998, Noumea, New Caledonia.

Waldron VR & Kelley DL, *Communicating Forgiveness.* Los Angeles, Sage Publications, 2008

Windham J, *Six O'Clock Saints* (1934), *More Saints for Six O'Clock* (1935), *Saints who Spoke English* (1939), *Saints by Request* (1937). Sheed & Ward, London

Glossary

In Aotearoa New Zealand Māori is an official language, and many words are in common use.

karakia	prayer, prayers
kete	carrier bag woven from flax
kōhanga (reo)	pre-school education in Māori context, language nest
koro	grand-father
koru	coiled stage of fern
marae	community centre
Papatūānuku	Mother Earth
pāua	iridescent shell, abalone
poroporo	plant with purple flowers
Rangi, Ranginui	Sky Father
rangiora	large-leaved plant
tamariki	children
taonga	treasure/s
tikanga	customs, lore
tūī	native bird wide range of song sounds
wairua	spirit, Spirit
whenua	earth, placenta. Māori traditionally bury a child's placenta at the home marae.

Acknowledgements

Sincere thanks:

To my fore-mothers in family and faith – you prepared the way for my life and my journey!

To those who have shared lives and ministries with me in potent, inclusive ways – you are honoured in these pages!

To those whose search for wholeness brings them to share their stories – you inspire and teach me!

To those who generously invited visits or suggested amazing expeditions – your initiatives were fruitful, thought-provoking and enjoyable!

To all who have shared their wisdom with me, and supported my various inner and outer explorations – you too are honoured here!

To the friends who have given material support to the project: Tony Pears, Anne Upton, Pat Booth, Veronica Leamy, Margaret Gwynn, Pauline Boyle, Lesley Young, John Broomfield and Jo Imlay – you are generous and wonderful!

To Stephanie Drew for another stunning design, and patience with multiple re-jigs, to Trish Harris for insightful and supportive editing, and to Susan Pryor for work on the original document and proof-reading – it has been a great team effort!

About the Author

Trish McBride was born in Lancaster, England and came to Aotearoa New Zealand in 1952. For most of her life she was deeply involved in the Catholic Church. She has subsequently spent times with ExAlt, a women's spirituality group, a Progressive Presbyterian parish, and the Religious Society of Friends, and now identifies as post-denominational.

Now retired, Trish has been a spiritual director, chaplain in various contexts, counsellor and supervisor. She is mother to 7 and delighted grandmother to 23, some acquired, and is now (2024) happily settled in a retirement village.

A high point in her writing career was as a prize-winner in a 1994 international competition for religious journalism awarded by *The Tablet,* London. Others have been contributing chapters to five Aotearoa Catholic-based theology books, (*The God Book, A Thinkers Guide to Sin, Journeying into Prayer, But is it Fair?* and *Living in the Planet Earth*), publication of two academic papers in USA, and completing her own unintended trilogy: *Faith Evolving, Exploring the Presence* and *A Love Quilt.*

Many of the articles and poems in her books have previously appeared in a variety of publications. Formal studies included MA (Hons) in Classics, Diploma in Pastoral Ministry and Recognition as an Associate in Christian Ministry (interdenominational).

Involvements include family, social justice, nurturing friendships, quilting, reading, swimming, walking and occasional painting.

About the book

Exploring the Presence: More Faith Patches is the passionate, rich and honest spiritual journey of a woman who left her church after awakening to the Divine Feminine. In her sequel to *Faith Evolving,* Trish McBride honours the Presence of the Holy One who permeates All that Is, however we may name Her / Him, in an authentic expression of women's spirituality.

The diversity of prose and poetic pieces of writing is 'quilted' together with a clear and concise voice. It is challenging and provocative in places, but also mellow and joyous, conveying the darkness and the light of the spiritual path. It claims continuity with the essence of the Catholic Christian tradition while exploring far and wide beyond. There is a sharing of the intimate details of a spiritual journey, attention to the texture of place, time and Spirit, an ability to convey the 'feel' of experiences and travels, and delight in the company of others on the Way.

Trish's honesty, integrity and ability to reflect on her own experiences make this book a good read, either as a whole, or a piece at a time. Readers interested in the contribution to faith of 'mind' as well as 'heart' will find this a rich resource. All of life is sacred!

Praise for Exploring the Presence

"This is a passionate and courageous book. Trish McBride shows us her soul as she invites us to journey with her and her friend Jesus, from the rich warm memories of the Catholic books and liturgy of her childhood to a broad and open place where she finds Godde in all things. The section 'Thinking it Through' has particular value. She raises and puts into a wider, sometimes surprising perspective many of today's questions. Through inner and outer journeying she explores the mystery of Godde through personal reflection, story, poetry, pilgrimage, play and many other ways discovering in the midst the Sacred Feminine, so enriching to her life. As the old secure images of God crumble this book will help many discover new depths and meaning."

Marg Schrader, Spiritual Director

"Trish McBride's brave and creative book deserves a wide audience. She is a fearless spiritual explorer dedicated to making sense of her own journey and the world around her. With a faith that is genuinely life-giving and liberation-focussed, she travels everywhere across the planet, across religious and spiritual traditions, across ethnic and gender divides. 'Faith seeking understanding' can and must go in any direction!"

Mike Fitzsimons, Writer and Publisher

"Those who loved *Faith Evolving* will welcome Trish McBride's invitation to continue with her on her deeply personal journey, 'holding the hand of Jesus', to times and places where, as a woman, she could worship in her own language, her own culture!"

Dr John Broomfield, Former President,
California Institute of Integral Studies

Books by Trish McBride

Trish's three books – *Faith Evolving, Exploring the Presence* and *A Love Quilt* – are being republished in 2024. Read together, they document Trish's 75-year life and faith journey from childhood to her 80s – a unique longitudinal record of women's spirituality and thinking. They are both spiritual biography and contextual theology.

Along the way, Trish moves from a traditional Catholic faith to embracing feminist theology and on into a post-denominational, inclusive, integrated Gospel-centred spirituality. She has used a patchwork metaphor across all three books, connecting writings of many colours, shapes and textures. Her purpose in all three has been to encourage others to ponder and record their own faith journeys.

Available in Print and as eBooks (in PDF, ePub and Kindle-Mobi formats)
Order Trish's books at: www.philipgarsidebooks.com

Faith Evolving: *A Patchwork Journey*
3rd edition – Republished – 2024

How is religious faith affected by our life's experiences? Trish McBride started with a traditional Christian faith, which evolved into a belief in a God who is free of denominational boundaries. The various 'patches' of 30 years of life-faith poems, prayers and stories have become a compelling story that will touch your heart and invite reflection.

Exploring the Presence: *More Faith Patches*
Republished – 2024

The passionate, rich and honest story of a woman who left her church after awakening to the Divine Feminine. Trish honours the Presence of the Holy One who permeates All that Is, however we may name Her / Him, in an authentic expression of women's spirituality. A fearless spiritual exploration of other ways of knowing.

A Love Quilt: *Later Faith Patches*
Republished – 2024

A compilation of later-life writings from Trish's 75-year spiritual journey, blending Christian spirituality and unorthodox ideas on matters such as love, inter-faith, race, social justice, and science. Stories, poems, and liturgies to inspire you on your journey, encourage you and provoke thoughtful reflection.

www.ingramcontent.com/pod-product-compliance
Lightning Source LLC
Chambersburg PA
CBHW081002140626
46546CB00018B/2931